Just Another Pile of Stones

(The story of a solo peak bagger)

by

Christine Shepherd

Christine Shepherd

X

The Conrad Press

Just Another Pile of Stones

Published by The Conrad Press in the United Kingdom 2023

Tel: +44(0)1227 472 874

www.theconradpress.com

info@theconradpress.com

ISBN 978-1-916966-09-3

Typesetting and Cover Design by: Levellers

The Conrad Press logo was designed by Maria Priestley.

Printed and bound in Great Britain by Clays Ltd, Elcograf S.p.A.

For Albert and Henrietta with love.
May you enjoy many adventures of your own.

Cairn: -
a mound of rough stones built as a memorial or landmark, typically on a hilltop or skyline

Just Another Pile of Stones

Chapter 1.
It started on The Ratty

I heaved my suitcase up the hill from the main line station to reach the famous Ravenglass and Eskdale miniature railway. I was ten and had no idea of the spell that the Lake District would cast over me during the next seven days.

I climbed aboard The Ratty which looked impossibly small after the trains that had brought me and my family; Mum, Dad, my sister, Gillian, and Dad's mum, my diminutive Granny Kay, from Bolton to the Western Lake District. With a friendly whistle, we made our way into the magical valley of Eskdale. What do I remember from that journey? Wet, green ferns curling and unfurling; dripping from the recent rain but steaming slightly in the summer warmth. To this day when I think of that holiday, I think of those iconic plants that dominate the route of The Ratty. That first day, I learnt what green smelt like

We were heading for a guest house in Boot for our first CHA holiday.

In these days of child protection and safeguarding, it would be hard to explain the concept of holidays with The Countrywide Holiday Association (Formally, The Cooperative and Communal Holiday Association) but I thought it was wonderful. There is a plaque on the ascent of Catbells to commemorate the founder of the CHA; Thomas Arthur Leonard. I guess that without him, my life may have been very different.

On a CHA holiday, you arrived at a warm and comfortable guest house to be met by a friendly host whose job was to make you feel welcome and introduce you to other guests.

Meals were communal and there was dancing or games most evenings; table tennis tournaments and board games were usually organised by the host or any of the guests that had such an inclination. One evening in the week saw an impromptu concert with guests showing off their talents.

During the day there was a choice of walks which were graded A-C, (A being the most strenuous), or you could do your own thing. There was no obligation to stay with your parents. Each morning, you simply chose from a list of walks or activities and went off with whichever group suited you. Many of the children stuck together in friendship groups, formed quickly in the annex where families with children were housed.

In the early summer of 1970, we arrived at Stanley Ghyll House and disembarked to be greeted by friendly CHA members who would be our companions for the duration of our holiday. Throughout the week, we ate heartily, laughed, sang, walked and danced with those people who quickly became friends.

I remember forming a friendship with a Scottish girl called Anne. Her family fascinated me. There were five children, all with two Christian names. There is nothing uncommon in this except that their mum used one of their names and their dad the other; they said there was no point giving a child a name unless you used it!

That week I fell in love with The Lake District.

There were armfuls of wild flowers to collect and identify; (not recommended nowadays), trails to follow up to magical tarns, and rocky hills to climb. I have a very happy memory of sitting on a wet Green Gable eating soggy sandwiches while sheltering under Anne's dad's giant, black umbrella. Gortex hadn't been invented and most of us probably had our everyday anoraks on but that umbrella kept us dry. It is something I can't say it have seen very often on the fells.

These were early days of fell walking in terms of specialist clothing; footwear was heavy leather boots for some, stout lace ups or wellies for others. Outerwear varied considerably too, bike capes, car coats and anoraks but none of the bright yellow and orange waterproofs that were to make an appearance a few years later. I have a memory Granny sitting by Blea Tarn above Boot in wool coat and velvet hat, having been persuaded by her grand-daughters to climb the steep hill behind the guest house. It was on that hill that I saw my first snake. It was a small grass snake disturbed from Its home in the bracken by our passing boots. It didn't worry me but simply added to the Narnian wonders of the Eskdale Valley.

I hadn't seen many fells through the mist and rain of that week but The Lake District had already begun to seep into my veins and at the age of ten I was in thrall to its magic

Twelve months later, I arrived in another valley, a paradise surrounded by high fells and watered by more rain than anywhere else in England; Borrowdale. This time I arrived not on a miniature train but on a school coach. Our camp had been set up for us before we arrived. Dozens of bell tents were spread out across the field that would be our home for a week. Eight pupils in each tent slept on itchy palliasses radiating out from the centre pole like spokes on a bike wheel. We ate uncomplainingly, in the mess tent on long tables, basic food that satisfied hunger created by fresh air and exercise.

On this holiday I learnt to canoe; doing Eskimo rolls in the clear freezing waters of Derwent Water and paddling along the river. This would now be called kayaking but in 1971, single vessels propelled by double ended paddles were canoes and those with two seats and single blades were kayaks; I'm not sure when all that changed but I still call my single seater a canoe; old habits die hard.

I am sure that I remember paddling down to Grange, however looking at the stony river bed there these days, it's hard to believe that there was ever enough water there to paddle so maybe my memory is playing tricks. What I do remember clearly was travelling in the bone shaker, our transport, to the lake. Our school had acquired an old ambulance, painted it orange and put a canoe rack on its roof. We sat on the bench seats down the sides or on top of canoe paddles and life jackets down the centre; wherever we could find a space in the aptly named Clockwork Orange. Health and Safety would have had a field day.

Again, I had breathed the enchanted air of The Lake District but my love of the fells was cemented in Grasmere the following year.

A fell walker is born August 1972 on Maiden Moor

Chapter 2.
A fell walker is born

Our family were due to have another CHA holiday in The Lake District, in Grasmere, at the end of August 1972. This time, Dad was due to be the host for the fortnight. This would mean him meeting and greeting the other guests and generally helping to organise the groups and activities for the time we were there. At the last-minute my mum and sister were unable to come with us as Gillian was awarded a place at a school with different holidays to mine. This meant that, from the minute we arrived at Forest Side, I was largely left to my own devices as Dad was so busy; for a new teenager this was bliss.

The first week I opted for mostly 'B' walks, which were a perfect way to discover the fells around Grasmere, and Dad was happy that I wasn't risking life or limb on the 'A' walks and perhaps more importantly for him, I wouldn't hold anybody up if I struggled. I didn't! I discovered that I adored climbing and scrambling up any hills that were on offer. Of course, 'A' walks crept into my itinerary during the second week.

I remember, very fondly, a walk leader called George who clearly sensed my connection with the landscape and would send me scrambling up a hillside to report on the view or to look for the onward path. When we stopped by a sparkling tarn one day, to eat our hearty CHA packed lunch, George suggested that I went in to bring him a flower that he could spot a few metres from the shore. I willingly changed into my costume beneath my newly acquired Peter Storm yellow cagoule, took a deep breath and swam in the cold clear water. I remember small shoals of silvery blue fish parting as I glided through the tarn without a care in the world. I brought George his flower which he happily identified. Whether he really wanted it or it was just a way of encouraging me to experience my first wild swim I'll never know, but I loved it. I guess I was swimming in Grisedale Tarn as when I passed that tarn, on a walk, a few years later it felt familiar but, on that holiday, I just ran, walked and climbed on mountains and swam in lakes and tarns without asking their names. I was just happy to be out experiencing as much as I could of a place that I sensed, even at that young age, was to be my spiritual home.

Helm Crag was one name I did learn that August. The short ascent of 'The Lion and The Lamb' was an afternoon walk from Forest Side. The majestic rocks watch over Grasmere like sentinels: silent and brooding but drawing every visitor's eyes heavenward, inviting them to climb to the craggy peak. This fell has felt the treads of my boots many times over the years. It was the first Lakeland summit that I encouraged my daughters to climb aged four and six and was the start of my first solo walk when, many years later, I set out consciously to 'bag The Wainwrights'. It was also to feature in the last walk of that particular list when I climbed to my final summit. Steel Fell was chosen so that I could descend over the hill that started it all.

I owe George an enormous debt of gratitude for giving me the freedom to explore the hills without reining in my enthusiastic wanderings whilst, I am sure, watching me and others and keeping us safe. I pity young people these days whose natural exuberance has to be curtailed because of over-zealous legislation and reams of paperwork that make up that all-encompassing term; Risk Assessment. I am positive that George did all the risk assessment necessary for our walks. It came from experience on the fells and having a knowledge of them that no books could teach or legislation cover. I chose to dedicate my last Wainwright to him and to my dad, who died the year before I finished. Their names were the ones that I wrote on a piece of paper and pushed deep into Steel Fell's summit cairn. I hope that somehow, they know.

1973 saw a family move to a 17th Century Cottage on the West Pennine moors above Bolton. Although it was in many ways an exciting move, the cottage was difficult for a teenager. We often woke up to no running water and had to wash in water from the water butt outside. The cottage was cold; my bedroom was accessed by walking through my parent's room and the back door came in through the bathroom; not ideal when you were in the bath and someone wanted to come in. However, there were advantages for a budding walker.

There were numerous walks from the front door. I could walk over the moors collecting delicious whinberries, walk up to Winter Hill Mast, explore Lord Leverhulme's Chinese Gardens or in summer, when I got up early enough, I could walk to school over the moors.

My favourite walk though, was up a hill called, Rivington Pike. This became my 'go to' hill when I was feeling down or moody as many teenagers feel from time to time. I would often set off in a foul temper announcing to everyone that I was, 'off up the Pike'. By the time I had walked along the rugged road above Anglezark reservoir and climbed to the top of the Pike, with its far-reaching views, the cobwebs had been blown away, my cheeks were rosy and my mood much improved. This walk was

A move to the country

also done one April Fool's Day when, unbeknown to my sister and myself, Dad had changed the clocks in the house so that we got up at 5:45am instead of 6:45. When we were dressed and ready, Dad announced that we were going up the Pike before school. I can't quite recall my feelings on that occasion.

I came to love the cottage and its surroundings; it was to be our family's home for the next forty-three years. In case you were wondering, we did have the back door blocked off!

My love of walking was growing. I bought a book which detailed walks around Bolton that could be reached by public transport. I conscripted different friends to join me on these walks, which took me to some beautiful places, none too far from home. That little book gave me a freedom which many young teenagers can only dream of today. In the back of the book was a list of useful organisations for walkers including, of course, the YHA. Dad had used Youth Hostels with his friend, Peter, when he was younger and his tales had whetted my appetite for trekking. I started to plan my first Youth Hostelling holiday.

Chapter 3.
Youth hostelling

Before I write about my hostelling experiences, anyone under forty may need an introduction to the Youth Hostels of the seventies. Today, people may use a Youth Hostel as a cheap hotel, knowing that they can sit down to a reasonably priced evening meal accompanied by a bottle of wine of their choice or maybe an aptly named

Wainwright beer. They can stay in a comfortable room with a few individually lit bunks and leave the next day without a backward glance.

Hostels were very different when I embarked on my first YHA holiday in 1974. You arrived at 5:00pm (not a moment before) to a warm welcome but not necessarily a warm hostel. You signed in and were given your room allocation and a sheet sleeping bag, (unless you had been very organised and made one from an old sheet to the specifications given in the YHA handbook, which you carried from hostel to hostel.)

If you wanted to have a shower to wash off the day's sweat and mud you might have had to put a five pence piece in a slot for hot water or press a button on the wall, (not inside the shower), which slowly made its way out again. As soon as your money ran out or the button was at its limit you were suddenly hit by a stream of freezing cold water which had you jumping out of the shower pretty sharpish. The squeals heard from the bathroom were frequent and loud! It did ensure that no-one hogged the showers though. Everyone chatted in the hostel lounge over nothing stronger than tea or orange juice; alcohol was forbidden on hostel premises. This was usually the only warm room, heated by a fire, tortoise stove, or storage heater. There was often a fog of smoke too as no smoking was only enforced in some hostels.

By ten o'clock, people were usually tucked up under grey woollen blankets in their bunks; tired after a day's walking or cycling; very few hostellers turned up in cars. At half past ten, if not before, 'lights out' was called. This meant the main room light was switched off. It was all or nothing in those days.

The next morning, after scrambling quickly into clothes in cold dormitories and collecting items left in the drying room overnight, (incidentally the musty, slightly sweaty smell of the drying room is something that hasn't changed over the last forty-five years!), you made your way to the warden to be given your hostel duties which had to be completed before you were free to leave. Some of these duties were fairly simple like brushing the staircase or dusting the windowsills but others were less welcome such as cleaning the sinks and toilets, or scrubbing kitchen pans with Brillo Pads until they shone.

Once these were completed, you wrote in the hostel book your intended route for the day and your destination, on the understanding that you would ring the following evening to confirm your arrival. This feature was enormously comforting to my parents, knowing that someone was looking out for my welfare. I am pleased to report that when I hostelled solo a few years ago, the warden was happy to take a note of my route and ETA back at my car though there wasn't a book left out for this specific purpose as there used to be.

I daresay wardens wouldn't be able to allocate 'hostel duties' these days without checking a list of allergens on the cleaning materials or writing a risk assessment to cover themselves in case someone happened to fall downstairs while using an unquestionably dangerous dustpan and brush. It's a pity though that the 'improvements' in hostels have resulted in them being almost as pricey as bed and breakfast establishments and beyond the reach of young teenagers with a limited budget.

Aged fourteen, I organised a week's holiday in the Lake District with a good friend. I selected hostels and planned the routes between them. There was no internet in those days so I sat down with a pad and paper and wrote to the hostels, enclosing postal orders to pay for our accommodation. Hostels were cheap enough in 1974; about fifty pence a night in a simple hostel, and we could easily pay for a holiday with savings from pocket money.

In the Easter holidays of 1974, my friend Alison and I were waved off by incredibly understanding parents as we caught a coach to Whitehaven and from there, a train to Ravenglass to catch the Ratty for a second time into Eskdale, where my love of the Lakes had begun almost four years earlier. Looking back, Eskdale probably wasn't the most sensible place to start from. It was just that I wanted someone else to experience that wonderful valley.

I had learnt to use a compass in The Guides and I carried a one-inch tourist map on which I had worked out the routes between hostels. In the YHA handbook it said Coniston Coppermines was ten miles away from Eskdale, which sounded fine.

That first day we walked over bridges, stone hopped across streams and plodded across wet fields to Birks Bridge before walking the fell road to Coniston. I think I nearly lost a friend that day; the seemingly endless miles over the Walna Scar Road had taken its toll. When we realised that we had an uphill walk to the Coppermines Hostel in failing light, we broke an unspoken promise that we had made to our parents and hitched a lift. We had made it.

Walking into the hostel lounge after a shower and change of clothes, we felt refreshed and quietly satisfied with ourselves. We were greeted by a strange exotic smell from the Gauloises cigarettes of a group of French hostellers. My Dad had smoked cigarettes and a pipe when I was little, but this aroma was something spicy and foreign. I was experiencing a new world. I am not advocating smoking and have never smoked myself but it was something I remember so clearly that whenever I smell French cigarettes, I am taken back to that first day of new found independence.

The other memory that I carry with me about Coniston Coppermines was a little less pleasant. The girls' dorm had iron bunk beds and a slate floor. The night was cold and the hole in the door let in the night air which rendered iron and slate into blocks of ice. I yelped as my bare feet touched the floor the following morning; I don't think my feet had ever felt such cold.

The holiday continued without too many dramas as we walked into the tourist hot spots of Hawkshead and Ambleside.

Ambleside Hostel was my least favourite hostel of the week mainly because it was, in my mind, too big and too busy. However, it was very modern by 1974 standards. It even had a disco in its cellar. It was a huge contrast to the peace and quiet of the Western Lake District to be dancing to the rasping tones of Suzi Quatro's,' Devil Gate Drive'. Ambleside was also the first hostel to use duvets. It took quite an effort to keep mine on the top bunk when I was used to tightly tucked in blankets.

The following Easter, I was eager to hostel again. This time, I walked with a friend I had made in the Guides. Janet and I started and finished at a hostel that would become one of my favourites: - Grasmere Thorney How. The hostel always had a lovely atmosphere and those who visited it will have, on their membership cards, the cute little owl which was Thorney How's stamp. I visited this hostel many years later in 2010, just before it became an independent hostel in order to climb my penultimate Wainwright, Tarn Crag, Easedale. I bought a postcard as a memento and I had it stamped with the owl; unchanged after thirty-five years.

Thirlmere was another memorable hostel from 1975. This was heated by an old- fashioned tortoise stove in the corner of the communal sitting room and lit by gas lamps. The warden, who incidentally made the most delicious flap jack, knocked on the girls' dorm at 10:00pm, (lights out time) and then came in, climbed up on the bottom rung of each necessary bunk bed in turn, to reach up to turn out the gas lights, (Probably not the safest of lighting solutions in a hostel built primarily from wood).

I also remember being exhilarated by the climb up Sticks Pass from Thirlmere which cemented my love of steep ascents. I still prefer it to a slow slog to a summit.

My third year of hostelling was the last of conscripting friends to walk with me. I don't think my choice of routes over steep passes and rough terrain suited anyone except me. It is a measure of my love of walking and of the amazing Lake District, that I can remember the routes I walked in 1976 and details about the hostels I stayed in but I have wracked my brains and searched my memory and cannot for the life of me remember the name of the person I hostelled with in 1976. Sorry, whoever you were!

Now, when I am walking the fells, I take dozens of digital photos to remind me of my trip. However, occasionally there is a view which imprints itself onto my mind in a way that needs no photograph to recall it. One morning during Easter of 1976 I experienced such a view. We were lucky enough to be staying at the fabulously remote Black Sail Hostel. When the warden brought pitchers of water for our morning ablutions, he told us to come outside as soon as we could. We pulled on warm jumpers and made our way out into the freezing spring air. We were greeted by a magnificent sunrise that filled the sky and lit up snow on The Haystacks so that the summit glowed with a soft orange light. Below us, in the valley, the morning cloud lay thick and white. The pine trees poking through the inversion, looked like a scene on a Christmas cake. That view is as clear today in my mind today as it was on that wonderful morning.

Another memory, that has been triggered by writing about my early experiences of hostelling, is of Vesta Curries purchased from the hostel shop for about fifty pence for two servings. These were dried meals that you reconstituted with water into deliciously salty concoctions. With the wonderfully varied Indian menus that are available today, these boxed wonders would probably taste disgusting but our palettes were a lot less discerning in the 70's and, after bland school dinners, they tasted amazing.

Chapter 4.
Going solo

It was to be four years before I hostelled again. I had A levels and college work to do and had to use holidays to earn some money to supplement my grant.

In the summer of 1980, I decided to go hostelling solo. I had finished my third year of college and didn't know whether I would be going back to continue to do my honours degree or would be catapulted into the world of work; this was dependent on results to be revealed in the middle of July. I had also just finished a four-year relationship, so was truly free. I needed some time to myself and felt that my beloved Lake District would give me the head space and healing that I needed. I planned a crazy two-week itinerary. I was to cover over one-hundred and twenty miles of walking during the fortnight and visit all the hostels, in the Lake District section of the YHA handbook, that I hadn't stayed at previously.

In spite of the three hostelling holidays, I had planned previously, I was still pretty naïve. Using only the hostel handbook for reference, I decided that, after catching the coach to Windermere, my first night would be spent in the Duddon valley at Black Hall Farm and I would spend the fortnight making my way back to Windermere taking a circuitous route around the Lake District.

I had looked in the hostel handbook which assured me that The Mountain Goat bus service ran from Windermere to Duddon. However, what I hadn't realised was that, the Mountain Goat is not a regular bus service that you can wait for and catch to your required destination. It is a company providing sight-seeing tours around The Lake District. At the start of my holiday, I was in Windermere needing to get to Black Hall Farm before nightfall. I took out my tourist map and 'Youth Hostels in Lakeland', book (This was a publication that gave routes between Lakeland Hostels), and worked out that if I caught a bus to Ambleside, I could follow the route from there to Elterwater and then the route from Elterwater to Duddon. It was going to be a nine-mile walk and it was already well past mid-day. However, I didn't really panic as I knew I was capable of doing the walk and in late May, daylight was stretching out late into the evening. Mind you, it wasn't the way that I had planned to spend my first day.

I got off the bus in Ambleside and walked out of the busy town to join the Langdale to Coniston Road. By 1980 I was more aware of how unsafe it was to hitch a lift, (however tempting it might have been), so before entering the path to Loughrigg Terrace, I stopped to have a drink and check my map again, with no intention of getting a lift. However, I was suddenly aware of a car slowing to a halt in the lay-by just ahead of me. The window of a battered old Volvo was wound down and a lady's head popped out and she called out to me. I went cautiously towards the car to be greeted by a friendly smile and an equally friendly voice asking for my advice. There were three children in the back and various drinks cans and sweet packets littering the floor of the car, suggesting the family were having a fun day out. It turned out that it was the first time they had visited The Lake District and their aim was to see as much of the area as possible. They wanted to know if I knew anything about the Western Lakes. I told them that I loved Eskdale and that I was actually heading for the Duddon Valley.

They couldn't believe that I was intending to walk there, so I told them my sorry tale. Immediately, they decided that they fancied seeing the quieter area of the Lakes that I had described and offered to take me to my destination. I am a Christian and don't believe in luck so I guess I would say that there was an angel looking out for me that day. As if to drive that point home, there was a small bible in the storage space between the front seats. I hadn't hitched but did get a lift. I arrived at the hostel, Black Hall Farm, in good time and the Lake District newcomers had experienced the beautiful remoteness of the South Western area. I don't know where they decided to head next or whether they decided to risk The Hardknott and Wrynose Pass for their return journey, but I hope they have been back to The Lake District many times since.

I spent the next day exploring the Duddon Valley and revelling in the knowledge that I had a whole fortnight in which to drink in the elixir of my favourite place in the world with no-one to question my choice of routes or pace and only myself to worry about. That may sound selfish but it was more the sense of relief that I felt in not having to second guess what my companions were thinking about me and my navigation or worrying that I may lead them into danger. I was free to find out what I was capable of and, as it turned out, my limitations.

I was still only using the one-inch Tourist map, which incidentally I still own. Although I now use the much more detailed OS maps when I am walking, I can see that there were some advantages in using the Tourist map. For one thing, I could see the whole of the Lake District in one go and for another, only the really good footpaths and tracks were shown. This ensured that the walks I did were relatively safe and not too much off the beaten track.

The main disadvantage was that it lulled me into a false sense of security in that the distances between hostels looked very short and manageable. My planned tour was to take in every corner of that map from The Duddon valley to Kendal in the South and Patterdale to Cockermouth in the North. This was an ambitious itinerary especially considering the weight of my rucksack. Looking back, I realise that my large pack must have weighed a ton.

The modern inventions of micro-fleeces, pack towels and waterproofs that fold up in their own pockets, mean that water is the heaviest item that hikers in the 2020s carry. In 1980 my rucksack, which had a surprisingly comfortable, external aluminium frame, was stuffed with clothes for a fortnight and included, unbelievably, a hand-knitted Aran sweater for cold days and a bath towel.

As I look at the hostel stamps on my YHA card I struggle to remember my exact itinerary but there are plenty of incidents that still feel as fresh in my memory as when they happened in 1980.

I walked from Black Hall Farm over to Hawkshead via Coniston. As I walked towards Hawkshead, the heavens opened and I donned my bright orange, Peter Storm, cagoule and over-trousers and drew up the hood cord round my face. I must have been grinning to myself as I walked along as I was stopped by a couple who asked if they could take my picture. They said they couldn't believe that someone could be so wet and look so happy. I asked them if they would mind taking a picture on my point and shoot camera which they did. This is one of the only photos I have of my solo tour of 1980 but it is a treasured reminder of that holiday.

On this holiday I climbed the wonderful Langdale Pikes for the first time. I hadn't climbed to many summits with the friends on previous holidays but on this one I had no-one to stop me. The weather wasn't particularly kind and I didn't get the fine views that I was hoping for but I enjoyed the rugged scramble up Pike O' Stickle, in spite of one heart-stopping moment when a gust of wind caught my large and cumbersome rucksack and nearly spun me off the fell. Incidents like this have happened quite frequently over the years and, far from putting me off climbing solo, they somehow add to the feeling of achievement and satisfaction at the end of the day. The wind must have been fairly strong for a couple of days as I also remember having to hunker down on Ore Gap waiting for the winds to ease as I could hardly stand up without being blown off course.

Cockermouth Hostel was on the fringes of the Lakes but I was glad that I had added it to my holiday. It was a lovely hostel, with its own water wheel as I remember. There were only six of us spending the night there and were all intending to cook for ourselves. As luck would have it though, one of my fellow hostellers had had a successful day's fishing in Ennerdale and carried a huge pike into the kitchen. This was gutted and cleaned by us all, fried in butter and then shared out to be sandwiched between slices of home-made bread. If the Haystack's view imprinted itself on my visual memory, then that fresh pike did the same with my taste-buds. It was the most delicious fish I have ever eaten.

The day after that memorable meal, I walked to Ennerdale without another soul for company. I had been walking for fourteen days and my boots were starting to rub my big toe. I think I would have been fine but for the long plod up the Ennerdale Valley to the hostel hidden in the trees. I knocked and went into a very quiet hallway. The warden met me with the news that I was the only person staying that night. After the camaraderie of the previous evening, I suddenly felt very lonely and very sore. Unfortunately, when I phoned home, my mum could hear in my voice that I wasn't as happy as I had been on previous nights and as mums are capable of doing, she made me feel quite emotional. She decided, in spite of my protests, that she and Dad would drive up to The Lakes the next day and pick me up. I had reached my limit. I wish I had carried on as I was due to stay at the wonderful Black Sail again that night but I guess with a blistered toe, a heavy pack and over a hundred and twenty miles under my belt, it was time to call it a day. It wasn't the way I wanted my adventure to end but it some ways it was fortuitous as it left me wanting more. I had also had my first taste of 'bagging'. I had visited every hostel in The Lake District. I enjoyed the feeling of completion, a feeling that I was to replicate several times over thirty years later.

Chapter 5.
Walking takes a back seat

After College, there was little time for mountains as I moved to Leeds, began my teaching career, and met and married my husband, Peter.

We did spend a couple of days in the Lake District for our honeymoon and I introduced my husband to one of my favourite places up to then, Grisedale Tarn, above Grasmere, but we didn't really do any serious walking. Peter had said that he liked walking when we met but I don't think that he was quite prepared for what I meant when I said that I liked to walk!

Over the next few years, we settled into family life, having two beautiful daughters in 1986 and 1988. I was eager to get Hannah and Rebecca into the great outdoors, but as my husband worked shifts and I didn't drive, most of our outdoor adventures were in local parks; going on 'mud hunts' and feeding ducks. I had a break from teaching, and to bring in the pennies, I became a childminder. It was a busy few years and mountains had to be enjoyed vicariously by watching videos and reading books.

In 1992 I missed a chance to do the National Three Peaks with a group of friends. I was starting to plan for this when I unexpectedly became pregnant and soon after, sadly suffered a miscarriage. The National Three Peaks remains a challenge that I haven't ever undertaken.

When Rebecca was four, I went back to teaching, doing a few days' supply when I could fit it in with the girls' schooling. I had also passed my driving test. This gave us the opportunity to go further afield. I remember our first proper walk was The Ingleton Waterfalls walk which we all enjoyed. I started to plan more walks. Of course, I wanted to encourage the girls to climb a 'mountain' as soon as possible.

Hannah and Rebecca's first Wainwright peak was, of course, Helm Crag, 'The Lion and The Lamb'. The girls were brilliant and I was thrilled to bits to be out on the fells once again. My husband was a bit worried as the light was fading by the time, we were walking back to Grasmere but I knew the path like the back of my hand and we were back in plenty of time. We stayed at Thorney How and the girls enjoyed their first experience of hostelling.

Peter and I did have a lovely weekend together in Coniston, without the children, (grandparents are amazing!), celebrating our tenth wedding anniversary in 1994. We climbed Coniston and I remember the turquoise of Lever's Water was the brightest I have ever seen it. I also remember walking backwards down Walna Scar Road back into Coniston as my toes were rubbing in my boots on the steep descent. Looking back, I can't quite believe that we only did The Old Man. All my visits since then have involved me walking several of the seven Coniston Fells; all too good to pass by.

I was beginning to get itchy feet and wanted to be out on those fells. In August 1997 I got my chance. Hannah's Godparents in Edinburgh offered to have the girls for a few days while we had a few days to ourselves. It was on this break that my poor husband finally learnt what I meant by, 'I love walking.' In anticipation I bought Colin Shelbourne's, 'Walker's Companion to the Lake District', with thoughts of some big mountains, and dreams of

Lakeland grit under my boots.

We had spent a lovely family holiday in Northumberland. Hannah and Rebecca had enjoyed lots of horse rides over the moors and had spent time jumping on and off hay bales in the farm where we were staying. On the Saturday, Peter drove from Haltwhistle to Edinburgh to drop off the girls and then down to the Kirkby Stephen for our mini break. Before turning in for the night, I reassured my husband that, as he had done a lot of driving, he could have rest day on the Sunday.

It wasn't to be! At 7:00am, Peter awoke to find me sitting up in bed with my map open in front of me. The hills were calling and I had to go. I'm still not sure how I did it but I persuaded him to agree to a walk. 'Let's just do Helvellyn today, 'I said, as though it was just going to be a gentle stroll in the park. We walked over Striding Edge and came back via Lower Man. I had had my fix!

We did have a rest day on the Monday, visiting Leven's Hall and going for a row on Windermere.

One day off was enough; I was ready for The Big One, Scafell Pike. It was a very hot day and we were both in shorts. The route in the book started the ascent from Seatoller and we joined quite a crowd. taking the same well- trodden path. Before our final ascent we had our sandwiches at the foot of Broad Crag which I decided to climb while Peter was enjoying a more leisurely lunch. We then made it to the summit of Scafell Pike without a problem. Though the views were a bit hazy, it was a great feeling to be on top of England. We descended via Taylor Force Gill, leaving the crowds to go down the Corridor Route. It is a descent I have used several times since, as I love the surprise of seeing the long drop of the waterfall through the trees as you take the rather vertiginous path back to Seatoller. The cooling sound of the thundering falls was especially welcome on that hot day.

When Peter removed his socks back at the car, he discovered that he had acquired quite a nasty blister on his heel. He didn't think he could wear his boots for another day's walking. Undeterred, I looked for another walk that he could do in his trainers. Skiddaw seemed to be okay. Poor Peter! He did agree to do Skiddaw after reading the walk description. It wasn't the easiest walk but we set off in good spirits. Unfortunately, we walked into the cloud. The moisture from the clouds on the dry slate scree made the route very slippery but we were young and we laughed as we sang and slipped in the mist. We were rewarded for our efforts. As we emerged from the clouds on the descent, we were greeted by the most glorious rainbow and as we were marvelling at that, a buzzard opened its wings, majestically framed beautifully by the bow. It was the perfect end to our day's walking and to our mini break.

My desire for the hills had been ignited by this brief holiday and, as the girls were growing up and were happy to stay at home with their dad while I went off walking, I was able to fit in the occasional walk with a friend who also enjoyed the hills. In the spirit of completion, I decided to finish all the walks in the book that Peter and I had used to climb Helvellyn, Skiddaw and Scafell Pike.

One wonderful walk done in October 1998 was over St Sunday Crag and Fairfield. Autumn has always been my favourite time of the year to walk. I don't mind the cold when I'm walking and when the air is clear, the views can be spectacular. This was one of those days. We had an amazing day and as we made our way back through the beautiful Deepdale Valley, we were treated to the sight of a red squirrel frolicking though the red and golden trees. It had been a perfect walk. Then we got back to the car.

We were looking forward to the flask of hot coffee that we had left in the boot and to changing out of our boots, ready for the journey back to Leeds. As I went to open the boot, I realised that something was wrong. The lock had been forced. Our coffee and our trainers had been taken. Sadly, for my friend, the thieves had also taken an old jumper that she had left in the boot. This was of great sentimental value as it had belonged to her son who had tragically lost his life a couple of years before. It was so sad that such a glorious day had been spoilt. My boots were too heavy to drive in so I had to drive back to Leeds in my socks, which was far from ideal.

Chapter 6.
Walking with the family

Growing up, our girls were both members of Leeds Asthma Swimming Club; both Rebecca and myself have the condition. This wonderful club had been given a sum of money from Children in Need which was to be spent on encouraging children with Asthma, and their families, to push themselves physically in a safe atmosphere, where their needs were understood and catered for, (the leaders carrying a nebuliser and oxygen, just in case).

The girls and I had the chance to go on a couple of camping weekends in the Lake District with the club; Peter often had to work weekends. The first year, we camped in the glorious Langdale Valley and walked up Bow Fell on a scorching hot day. I loved it and the girls aged nine and ten, managed the walk without any problem. Hannah even wrote a lovely report about her achievement.

The following year, Hannah chose to stay at home, but

Rebecca and I enjoyed another weekend with the Club. The big walk that year was Pike O'Blisco and Crinkle Crags. The weather wasn't wonderful, very wild and windy at times and as we approached Crinkle Crags, Rebecca, the youngest on the walk, had to sit down to prevent herself from being blown off the path. With a strong hand either side from myself and another club member, Rebecca continued happily and enjoyed a feeling of satisfaction when she met someone on The Band, who asked how far she had walked and was very surprised when she told them where she had hiked and that she was only ten.

I think that walk probably made a hiker of her and we were to share lots of lovely walks together over the next few years.

The girls were, and still are, as different as chalk and cheese. In their teenage years these differences became more marked. They have always been really good friends but their ideas of how they wanted to spend their leisure time varied considerably. Peter and I solved this dilemma by giving them special weekends occasionally, when I would take one of the girls away and Peter would entertain the other at home. Hannah had inherited my love of reading and the arts and I spent lovely weekends with her in Stratford, going to the theatre and visiting stately historic houses and as Rebecca was emerging as a good walker and climber, our weekends were spent hiking.

In 1999 Peter, an occasional long- distance runner, started experiencing health problems. He used to run around a local park while training for a marathon or half marathon. More and more often, he was coming in from these runs with muddy knees and bloody shins and hands from a trip or fall. After buying new shoes, in case these were the problem, to no avail, he went to the GP.

This was the start of a medical mystery that took twenty years to solve. Initially, it was thought that Peter had a slipped disc. He was told to stop running for a while so that he could have scans and be treated. If only it had been that simple!

I didn't go walking for a while as it seemed cruel to be pursuing my hobby while Peter couldn't pursue his.

Ruling out a slipped disc, Peter underwent a barrage of tests and investigations. Meanwhile his mobility was deteriorating. Not knowing how bad things were going to get, we moved house in 2002. We did some local walks to explore the area. Occasionally, a stile or big step would prove a huge obstacle for Peter and he would have to lift his foot with his hands. At other times he coped well. However, proper hiking together was out of the question. I did the occasional walk with Rebecca but, as she was a teenager with a busy social life, we didn't get out as often as I would have liked.

It was on one of these precious walks, when Rebecca and I had reached the summit of Helvellyn on a lovely summer's day climbing via White Side and Raise, that I looked at the glorious view; mountains and fells reaching out in every direction, and made a decision. It was coming up to my forty-sixth birthday and I said to Rebecca, 'I am going to try and make sure that I have climbed the highest fifty mountains in The Lake District before I am fifty. '

Chapter 7.
The challenge begins

The highest fifty; that sounded simple but then I found that there were various lists. As I was already acquainted with The Wainwrights, thanks to Dad's copies of a couple of the Pictorial Guides, I decided that I would try to ensure had I bagged the highest fifty Wainwrights before I reached my half century.

Rebecca and a couple of friends accompanied me on several of my peak bagging days but I was still hoping Peter would get well and we could climb some together. This wasn't to be and with friends not always available, my progress was slow. It was at this point that Peter encouraged me to go solo. As he said, I had Youth Hostelled solo in my early twenties and I could read a map so why not give it a go?

My first solo walk started with my favourite, Helm Crag. I decided not to go too high until I had gained more confidence in my route-finding abilities. It was a cold day in the Easter Holidays and I drove up to the Lakes feeling a bit nervous but reassured by the familiarity of the first fell. I didn't have a very auspicious start as I happily walked along the track completely missing the steep path up the crag. After walking on for several minutes, I retraced my steps to the start of the ascent. I looked around me feeling rather shamefaced but realised that no-one had witnessed my mistake. I made my way to the summit in bright sunshine, the ground getting crisper and the air colder as I gained altitude.

I walked on from the summit to other fells, not meeting anyone. I was in my happy place. The views were wonderful, the sky was blue and the air was clear. My first solo walk for over twenty years had made me eager for more.

The following year, I resigned from my teaching post, following an unpleasant episode in my career, when I had experienced bullying and isolation. I started working for an agency as a supply teacher and Peter began receiving regular phone calls at work; 'The agency hasn't called; I am off to the Lakes'. On weekends when we could escape together, Peter got used to finding pleasant pubs and coffee shops in which to pass the time while I hiked up a fell or two.

I soon became quite confident in my ability to follow a walk route on my own but I was running out of walks in the books I owned. As walking books weren't cheap, I was wondering what to do next, when I became aware of a website called go4awalk; this was to change my life. I was suddenly made aware of lots of lists, and fells that I had never heard of. I signed up and began downloading walks that took in several Wainwrights in a day's walking. I walked higher and further than I had ever done before.

In doing the highest fifty Wainwright's I was to have many memorable moments that I can remember today as clearly as if I had a video in front of me.

One wonderful day that I remember clearly was bagging the Coniston Fells. I put two routes together so that I could climb all the Coniston Fells in one round. I walked along the Walna Scar Road to Brown Pike and proceeded to scramble over the rugged peak of Dow Crag before taking in Brim Fell, Swirl How, Great Carrs, Grey Friar and of course, Coniston Old Man. I have since done this round twice adding on Wetherlam once as well. At the time of writing, I am thinking that it would be a good round to celebrate my seventieth birthday, seven fells; one for each decade. Whether I will still think it is a good idea when that significant day arrives is anyone's guess.

Climbing the highest Wainwrights, while challenging physically sometimes, is rarely a problem as far as route finding is concerned. The eroded footpaths are usually peopled with groups of walkers and I am rarely alone on these fells. However, one day was quite different. I had decided to climb Scafell via Lord's Rake. I set off confidently from Wasdale Head, sure of the route I wanted to take. Unfortunately, my plans were curtailed by a notice announcing a large rock fall on The Rake. This was no longer an option for the ascent. Using my map, I walked towards Burnmoor Tarn and took the direct path from there without incident. The weather was warm but it was humid and, with the heat haze, the summit was quite misty and ethereal and there wasn't another soul in sight. I decided to climb Symonds Knott as well, just because it was there. I was retracing my steps ready for the descent, when a voice shouted out from the mist, 'Hey! You!' I was a female, alone on a mountain with someone shouting quite aggressively at me.

Friends often worried about me walking alone in case I should meet some unsavoury character on the fell. I had always laughed; until this point. I stayed my distance and shouted back, 'Hi! Are you okay?', I got reply 'No! Do you know where we are?' Listening more carefully, I realised that, what I had taken for aggression was, in fact, fear.

I approached the man who was making his way towards me. It was obvious that he was holding his arm awkwardly and that he looked exhausted. It transpired that he had come up the same way as me and was intending to return to Wasdale Head via Lord's Rake.

This meant that he hadn't seen the sign and wouldn't have been aware of the new dangers as he began his descent. He had fallen and become disorientated. He had been struggling for nearly two hours and although he had returned to Scafell, he had no idea of his location. After giving him time to tell his tale in his lilting Welsh accent and take on some food and water, we began our descent, taking the straightforward route via Burnmoor Tarn. The descent is fairly steep in a couple of places and I could tell he was still in shock as he needed constant reassurance that I knew where I was going and he kept reliving his ordeal, saying that he had thought he was going to die on the rocks.

I did manage to lead him safely to the Wasdale campsite where he was staying and offered to get help but he said he would be okay. His parting shot made me smile though. He thanked me and said, 'You've been a real St Bernard today.' I think I would have preferred to have been called a guardian angel, rather than be likened to an enormous, slobbering member of the canine family. Still, it's the thought that counts.

There is a post-script to this story. A couple of years later my Mum was out walking on The West Pennine Moors and got chatting to a Welshman who said that he used to walk a lot in the Lake District until he had a bad fall and hurt his arm and that he had lost his way that day and it had shaken his confidence. Who knows? It might have been the same person.

Before I set out from home for a day's walking, I always check the mountain weather forecast and this has rarely let me down. One feature that is always guaranteed to have me packing up the car for an early start on the fells is the forecast for excellent visibility. I can cope with cold and rain but mist and fog can be dangerous even for an experienced walker and at this early stage of my peak bagging exploits, I certainly wouldn't have described myself as such. However, one February I looked at the forecast, not expecting much, to find a headline for the next day which said there would be excellent to superb visibility on the high fells and less than ten percent chance of rain. I was set for one of the most magical day's walking I have ever had.

I set off from Leeds about five thirty in the morning and by nine thirty was putting on my boots to set off walking beside Ennerdale Lake. As the winter sun rose higher in the sky, the trees beside Ennerdale sparkled and the frost on their needles began to melt. The air was crisp and clear and I made good progress. I had a thermal t-shirt on and soon became so warm that I could dispense of my jacket and walk unencumbered by too many layers.

I climbed steadily by a wall up to the summit of Caw Fell accompanied only by my own shadow. As I approached Caw Fell and Little Gowder Crag, I was joined by a few more walkers who had made their way up from Wasdale. The views were breath-taking. We were on rugged peaks which had a light dusting of snow to highlight every rock and crevice, the sky was a clear cornflower blue and to top it all we were looking at the peaks of the Scafell range peeping out from white clouds which had settled below us in the Wasdale Valley. We made our way to Haycock and about half a dozen hikers and a few dogs enjoyed what must have been the best lunch spot in England that day. It was February 6th and people were asking for sunscreen; the sun was so bright. The dogs were kept happy with snowballs thrown by their owners. I think we all felt that we were truly in paradise.

I then left the group to walk down over Steeple and

Long Crag back down to Ennerdale. The magic of the day was still making me smile but there was more to come. I walked back through a forest that the sun hadn't touch that day and which was thick with hoar frost. My feet crunched with every glorious step and the white trees and icicled stream made it look like a scene from Narnia and I half expected Mr Tumnus to pop out from behind one of the glistening pines. Although I had my gloves on at this stage, I still hadn't felt the need for my coat. Amazing! This was The Lake District in February. I emerged back out on to the lake side road after crossing the River Liza, just as the sun was beginning to set over the lake. I reached my car as darkness fell into Ennerdale Water and ended one of the most perfect day's walking I have ever had. I drove back to Leeds feeling that I had been truly blessed that day and it is one that will live in my memory long after my walking days are done.

Chapter 8.
Out of my comfort zone

Blencathra was one peak that I had often seen on my trips to the Lakes but had never climbed. Even though I had crossed Striding Edge without a problem, I had been put off by tales of people falling to their death from Sharp Edge or becoming 'crag fast' and having to be rescued. However, if I was going to complete my mission, it would have to be done, or so I thought. (I have since found many much safer routes up Blencathra.) Rebecca, by this time, quite an accomplished climber, volunteered to accompany me and 'help' me across.

On a cold bright spring day, we made our way up the fell from Scales. I had a short debate with myself about whether to risk Sharp Edge or take the longer and safer route up by the tarn. Rebecca was having none of it. She had come to do Sharp Edge and that was the way we were going. I spotted a slightly lower path as we approached the edge and assumed that this would be an easier path like the one on Striding Edge. This turned out to be a false hope and there was no choice but to cross the knife-like rocks. I am not a lover of heights and while Rebecca made it look like a Sunday afternoon stroll, I shuffled along, often sitting down, straddling the rocks, to make forward progress. Although Rebecca had left me to my own devices, I was reassured by the presence of a Mountain Rescue Team who were carrying out a training exercise on the most difficult section of the ridge. I still don't know if I would have made it across without their encouragement.

I have returned to Blencathra three or four times since this first ascent and on two occasions have reached the summit by the wonderful Hall's Fell Ridge which gives me the adrenalin rush that I enjoy without the feeling that death is imminent.

Unlike Blencathra, Lingmell doesn't really offer any problem on its ascent unless, as I did, you choose a day with horrendously strong winds and pouring rain. Lingmell was the last of the highest fifty Wainwright's that I had to climb. To be fair I didn't choose to walk on a bad day. Everywhere else in The Lakes and in fact most of England had fine walking weather. Peter had driven me up from Leeds and there had been no indication that I was in for a bad day. However, as we approached Wasdale, the clouds darkened and the wind whipped up the water on Wastwater. By the time we reached the car park, the rain was coming down in torrents. I wouldn't ever have set out on a long walk on a day like this but the path was clear and I was only going up and down by the same path and then we could celebrate.

As I donned all my waterproof gear, I watched another walker making his way up the fell. He was taking a very odd line for his ascent. He seemed to go forward almost at a run and then move left before stopping, walking sideways to the right and then repeating the sequence. Peter and I couldn't understand it. Anyway, I set off, leaving Peter to listen to the radio commentary of an FA Cup Match. I reached the steep grassy path that we had watched the walker on half an hour earlier and suddenly found myself copying his line up the fell and I understood. The only way to make my way against the wind was to run or to walk as quickly as possible. Eventually, when my stamina ran out, I was blown sideways and using my poles for stability, stood for a minute to get my breath back. I then carefully made my way back to the path and started again. I reached the large pyramidal cairn, hunkered down to eat my lunch before making my way back down the fell.

Peter, having had his lunch in a warm pub, was back in the car engrossed in the football. Looking like a drowned rat, I had to knock loudly on the window to attract his attention above the noise of the rain. I peeled off my waterproofs and we made our way to the pub for a celebratory drink. I had visited the summits of Wainwright's top fifty mountains. I had done it with fifteen months to spare and I had got a taste for peak bagging. When I totted up the fells I had climbed, I realised that doing the top hundred before July 2009 was feasible. I was officially becoming a peak bagger.

I was so happy to have a new target. For the next few

years, The Mountain Weather Information Service and go4awalk were probably the most visited sites on my laptop. I was still supply-teaching but any free days would see me getting up at the crack of dawn to drive up the A65 for my next adventure. I visited parts of The Lake District that I hadn't even heard of.

There is a lot of criticism of peak baggers as people who are only interested in ticking 'tops' off on a list and we are often told just to 'enjoy the walk'. To those critics I say, 'Give it a go'. You will find beautiful places, away from the crowds and see your favourite fells from new angles and experience views that will have your eyes brimming up with tears of joy. We probably enjoy the walks even more because we have an amazing sense of achievement as we near our goal.

I did indeed complete Wainwright's top 100 by my 50th birthday. My last of this particular list was Slight Side. I could actually have bagged this when I took the unexpected route to Scafell but hadn't realised how near it was that day. Besides, if I had, I might not have been able to help the injured walker. Things happen for a reason. This day, I met three lovely chaps on Slight Side who were making their way to Scafell Pike, (Not the easiest of routes). They were amazed when I told them about my mission. They too had a target. This was printed on their T-shirts; Three Men, Three Peaks, Three Years. They were doing the three national summits. They had climbed Ben Nevis the previous year and this year's hike was to take them to the highest point in England. As Wainwright says: -

'One should always have a definite objective, in a walk as in life-it is so much more satisfying to reach a target by personal effort than to wander aimlessly....life without ambition is...well, aimless wandering.' Alfred Wainwright.

I hope the three gentlemen achieved their ambition. I think Wainwright would have approved, though I doubt that he would have understood why they didn't want to climb every fell that they could see around them.

Of course, as you have probably guessed, I didn't stop at one hundred. The 214 was now an achievable aim and my peak bagging was gathering momentum. When you walk alone there is no-one to question you or rein in your ambitions. Peter saw the joy it gave me to be out on the fells and he enjoyed the fells vicariously through my pictures and tales. When he could join me in The Lakes, he was happy to spend the time discovering new country pubs and coffee shops with delicious cakes.

Chapter 9.
Close encounters

While walking on my own, I often meet lovely people to chat to for a few hundred yards or so. I am careful not to become an unwanted companion for too long. Often joining someone can alter their pace and your own and walking becomes an effort for both of you. However, there are some encounters that are more memorable than others.

One hot August day, I had dropped my daughter off for a week's camping in Windermere and decided to go down to The Langdales to climb the pikes the next morning. I didn't really expect to find a hostel place or bed and breakfast in August so had packed my tent. Unfortunately, there wasn't even a camping place available for a single tent on the official camp sites.

Luckily, I drove down to the New Dungeon Ghyll Hotel and discovered that they were allowing tents on their grounds and I was able to pitch my tent and look forward to the next day's climb. It was a glorious evening so I decided to explore my route and climbed up to the beautiful Stickle Tarn and sat down on the wall surrounding the tarn, listening to the gently lapping water, surrounded by the magnificent crags with the giant wall of Pavey Ark in front of me. (Little did I know that I would be climbing up the exciting scramble of Jack's Rake a few years later.) I read a few chapters of my book before making my way back to the campsite and settling in. I decided to go to the pub for a night cap and found a young singer with an acoustic guitar setting up outside the inn. I sat and listened to her lovely music for a while. Her closing song was one of my favourites and the sounds of Joni Mitchell's 'Big Yellow Taxi', followed me back to my tent. I had had a perfect evening.

The next day I awoke expecting to find another day of glorious sunshine only to discover that my tent was wet and I was looking at other tents through a thick mist. It was still warm and I had my car boot to store my wet tent in so I wasn't too worried. I knew that the mist was likely to burn off before too long; the forecast was good for later in the day. I had a bowl of cereal and a steaming mug of tea in the New Dungeon Ghyll. I was so pleased that I had walked the first part of my route the previous evening as it meant that I was happy to walk this in poor visibility. I set off on the steep path safe in the knowledge that I was going the right way. There were quite a number of people joining me on the path but the weather had definitely kept away the huge crowds that I would have expected on a bank holiday in August. The sun began to break through and the temperature rose. I stopped to have a drink and was caught by a small family. They asked me how far it was to Stickle Tarn as their little girl was getting a bit tired. I was able to give them some encouragement and promised them that it was a lovely place for the picnic they were intending having there, before they made their descent. I continued on my way and after a few hundred yards was aware of the male of the family racing up the path towards me. I stopped, assuming that I had dropped something from my pack. He reached me and said, 'Are you from Leeds?' when I said, 'Yes', he went on to check my address in the '80s. He did look familiar but I was amazed when he said that he had lived next door to us when he was a student. Indeed, Peter and I still had a mantle clock that had been gifted to us when he and his housemates moved out, to thank us for our help with their garden and for putting up with them. (They were actually a lovely hard-working group of trainee medics and dentists.) We were able to share some memories before he introduced me to his wife and daughter. I thought this encounter would be a one off but no, others were to follow to remind me that, 'It is a small world'.

I was very glad of another of these chance meetings.

I drove from Leeds to Borrowdale on a hot May day in 2009. The valley was thronged with tourists and, passing the large numbers of brightly coloured tents in Stonethwaite camp site, I expected to be accompanied on my walk by other mountain lovers. However, as I started to climb up Big Stanger Gill, I heard nothing other than the sound of running water and saw no-one for the next few hours. We hear about the fact that truly wild places are difficult to find in the Lake District. I felt that I had found one, as I climbed steeply, amid the sharp Hawthorns and craggy rocks, besides the tumbling stream. I was glad of the shade of the trees as I could feel the hot sun burning through my first application of sunscreen. I crossed the gill and emerged at the top of the ravine into a lonely looking plateau surrounded by a ring of higher fells.

I made my way to the rocky summit of Bessy Boot on Rosthwaite Fell and continued down towards the Tarn at Leaves. The Tarn was black in spite of the sun and the marshy ground and the long grasses and reeds made it look rather uninviting. I decided it was time for a breather and found a rock on which to enjoy my lunch. As I was sitting by the Tarn and looking at my onward path, heavy clouds started to gather and the sun was suddenly swallowed up without ceremony. The atmosphere changed and instead of enjoying the peace of the fells, I felt disquieted by the darkness of the water and the now forbidding looking fells ahead. I packed up my sandwiches quickly and made my way to Rosthwaite Cam, still visible, though becoming fainter by the minute.

The next summit gave me confidence in my route finding and allowed me to get a clear compass bearing. Dovenest Top is, thankfully, very distinctive. I took stock and carefully followed my compass to Combe Door Top and Combe Head, knowing that ahead of me was the great bulk of Glaramara, which was coming and going in the thickening mist. I felt very relieved when I approached its familiar summit, which previously, I had reached in glorious sunshine. However, my relief was short lived. I was alone and in heavy mist.

I donned my waterproofs and set off towards Allen Crags. At this point I was looking at my compass every few minutes as the path was not clear. I became aware that I didn't seem to be making any progress and indeed, realised that I was walking in circles. My compass had fixed on some magnetic rock and was spinning. Since this walk, I have kept a spare compass or two in my pack but I don't know if it would have helped on this occasion. I don't really panic in these situations but I was getting very frustrated and slumped down against the cairn to have a think. Then I heard voices below me and out of the abyss a small group of hikers emerged.

I sprang up and headed in their direction. In only a couple of hundred yards I was on the path and happily descending back to Borrowdale, via Allen Crags. The group were happy for me to stay with them and we were soon chatting and sharing our walking stories. I told them that, as well as bagging Wainwrights, I was doing a recce to see if this was a suitable walk for a church group that I would be leading the following month. On questioning me about this further, it turned out that they knew the church and in particular, one of the women who would be walking with me. As we came down into Seathwaite, where their cars were parked, they offered me a lift down to Seatoller and my own transport. By now it was pouring with rain and I gladly accepted. My sunscreen had stayed zipped in my rucksack. It was hard to believe that at the beginning of the day, I had been worried about sunburn.

One of my last Wainwrights was Lank Rigg, partly because of the long drive needed to reach it and partly because of this warning in book seven of Wainwrights pictorial guides;

'Lank Rigg is an outsider- too remote to be bothered about-Meeting another human is outside the realms of possibility. Die here, unaccompanied, and your disappearance from society is likely to remain an unsolved mystery.'

However, Lank Rigg had to be done if I was to tick off all 214 summits. I made an early start and, following my map carefully, reached a lay-by that I took to be Scaly

Moss; my starting point. Two walkers were just starting to make their way up the path near my parking spot, so I took the opportunity to speak to them and check that I had read my map correctly, before donning my boots and gaiters, (the ground looked rather boggy in places).

I set off alone about ten minutes after the other walkers on a good path to reach a metal gate. This led me off to the left to reach the summit of Grike. As I then made my way towards Crag Fell, I was aware of two figures coming towards me. These were the men I had spoken to earlier. They had missed the turning off to Grike so had come back to bag it. As I still had Crag Fell to climb, we worked out that we would be reaching the edge of the forest at about the same time. In view of Wainwright's warning, we decided to climb the final peak, Lank Rigg, together.

Indeed, we did reach the path into the trees at the same time and chatted as we walked. I discovered that the men didn't really know each other but had arrived simultaneously at the parking spot, intending to do the same walk, so had decided to pair up. They introduced themselves and eventually, I was asked where I had come from. When I said Leeds, one of the men said, 'Oh my brother lives in Leeds.' Now Leeds is a big place. However, as we continued the conversation it turned out that, although we had moved away from Leeds city centre seven years previously, his brother still lived there. Not only did he live in an area I knew well, he lived in a street we had lived in for nearly twenty years. On finding out his brother's name I couldn't believe the coincidence; not only did Peter and I know his brother and family; we had babysat for his children and attended the same church for over twenty years. For once Wainwright had been proved wrong. I daresay that doesn't happen very often but it certainly wasn't the lonely walk I had been expecting.

Chapter 10.
Mistakes and mishaps

As a solo walker, I have no-one to check my routes with and if things go wrong on a hike, I have to sort them out myself. While bagging the Wainwrights, I was mostly walking on clearly marked paths and there were often people around to consult with to check directions. However, I did make some silly mistakes; not realising for some time that White Side and Whiteside were different summits and similarly, planning a walk to High Raise Langdale when I was meant to be bagging High Raise Mardale in my top fifty list. Other mistakes have been harder to rectify.

While climbing Pillar from Wasdale Head in 2005, I took an unintended turn towards the High-Level Route across the Shamrock Traverse which, incidentally, I absolutely loved. The heart-in-the-mouth moment as one first looks down into Ennerdale was glorious. I didn't get the usual feet tingling nerves that I often feel when greeted by sheer drops but just felt enormously privileged to come across such an amazing view. It was after this wonderful moment that I must have missed an obvious path to the summit and found myself slipping and sliding on a steep scree slope.

I seemed to be making little progress; one step forward two steps back. I didn't want to go back as I wasn't in any particular danger but was struggling to go forward. To one side of the scree were some craggy looking rocks that would possibly give some purchase to my boots but weren't too inviting. They did seem to be the only way up though, so I shuffled across the slope towards them. Although I could scramble in places, I felt uneasy, knowing that if I fell, I might sustain a serious injury and that no-one knew that I had taken this accidental diversion.

Necessity is the mother of invention and I decided to put my walking pole to good use. I locked the pole, horizontally behind and between two large rocks and used it to pull myself up until I could anchor myself in a good place to retrieve it and put it between higher slabs of granite. In this way I slowly and surely pulled myself onto the wide-open summit of Pillar, emerging very close to the Ordinance Survey ring.

Imagine my surprise, after all that solitude and effort, to find another lone female unpacking her rucksack. I initially assumed that she was reaching for her packed lunch as I was looking forward to doing. However, what she unpacked was not a welcome cheese sandwich but a series of poles and a radio. She was a member of an amateur radio society aiming to transmit messages from the high places of Great Britain. We had a fascinating conversation about our ambitions before I left the summit for the rest of the Mosedale Horseshoe which I completed without further incident.

A more serious incident happened, not when I was alone, but with my friend Miriam who I had bagged St Sunday Crag with, a few years previously. We set off on a lovely September day in 2007 with the intention of climbing Snarker Pike and Red Screes and coming down the Scandale Pass back to Ambleside. As we were walking well and reached the pass in good time, we decided to go over Little Hart Crag, Dove Crag and Hart

Crag to Fairfield. We set off back to Ambleside down the western side of the horseshoe on good paths not expecting any drama. Miriam said something that I didn't quite catch. Without thinking, I turned to hear her more clearly and as I did, my boot found a large boulder and I flew dramatically forward trying to regain my footing, to no avail. I landed with a bang on the hard ground with a hard rock digging into my ribs. I tried to breathe and failed. Feeling sure that I had punctured a lung, I signalled to Miriam that I couldn't breathe. She did the only thing she could think of and thumped me on the back. The shock made me take a deep breath and with this breath came the realisation that I wasn't going to die on this very popular route.

I sat up and assessed my injuries. My elbow was bleeding and seemed to be slightly out of place. Although I was hurting all over, it was this injury to my arm that was worrying me as I was due to be driving back to Leeds after the walk. I managed to stand and decided that I was fine to carry on. I was walking quite gingerly, massaging my elbow as I walked. All of a sudden, the bone clicked back into place and as the bleeding had stopped, I thought I would be left with no more than a few bruises.

We made it back to the car and Miriam helped me off with my rucksack. I then tried to get into my seat! It was at this point that I realised that I had probably done more damage than I thought. We moved the seat as far back as it would go and tilted it until it was almost horizontal and I slid in before Miriam wound the seat back into place as slowly and gently as she could. I drove back to Leeds and to this day have no idea how I got out of the car at the other end. The next day I went to A &E where they confirmed what I feared; I had broken at least two ribs in my fall. This fall didn't put me off and Fairfield

Horseshoe is still one of my favourite rounds. I felt quite proud that I had managed to walk back with those injuries; I guess adrenalin helps at times like these.

The incident on Glaramara, wasn't the only time that I was caught out in mist. Coincidentally, it was also another May day when I found myself wandering aimlessly on Nether Wasdale Common. Peter and I were staying in Eskdale so that I could bag some of the Western fells. I chose to do the Greendale Horseshoe as it was a short walk and I would have time to spend with my husband at the end of the day.

Peter dropped me off in Greendale in bright sunshine. I was wearing shorts and plenty of sunscreen as the day was warm for early May. I made it easily to the summit of Buckbarrow where I paused for a few minutes taking in the wonderful views of Wastwater shimmering in the sunlight and the dramatic screes falling steeply into its depths. I started to walk towards Seatallan when, with very little warning, the sky darkened and I was being pelted by huge hailstones that stung the backs of my bare legs and prevented me from looking up at my onward route at all. I struggled to pull my waterproofs out of my rucksack as they were well buried, and donned these as quickly as I could. By the time I was clothed for the sudden wintery conditions the, 'clear path' in my route description had disappeared under a cold white layer of hail and sleet. As I was walking on a grassy common, the path had only been only a slight depression in the grass, made by the footsteps of Herdwick sheep and the occasional peak bagger. There were no landmarks to fix my compass on and, disoriented by the mist that had gathered due to the sudden change in temperature, I declared myself well and truly lost.

I occasionally sing to myself on the fells, 'Climb Every

Mountain and 'The Skye Boat Song' are two particular favourites along, with the hymn,' How Great Thou Art'. However, on this occasion I didn't sing. I shouted, 'I'm lost and I don't know what to do', into the surrounding cloud and clag.

Common sense then prevailed; I was supposed to be walking North East to Seatallan so I decided to set my compass South West to see if I could pick up the path that I had been on when I left the sunny summit of Buckbarrow. Sure enough, as I descended, the strata of hail became thinner and the common turned green again. A couple of meters from where I was walking, I spotted the grassy path that I had been following before the weather turned. I reset my compass to North East and walked on the path towards Seatallan once more, this time with my compass firmly in my hand not veering left or right but keeping the needle steady. After about half an hour or maybe even less, I saw a grey mass emerging from the featureless landscape. The trig point of Seatallan was a very welcome sight.

I sat down to have my well-earned lunch. My hair was wet with droplets of moisture from the cloud that was still enveloping me and I was a bit light headed from meandering about, beyond my usual lunchtime, but I was in good spirits. I took a bite of my sandwich, expecting the cheese and pickle to taste like the nectar of the gods as usual but I struggled to swallow even a morsel. It felt like cardboard in my mouth. I decided I must be thirsty and took on some water but again I struggled to down the liquid. I knew I needed to take on fuel but didn't know what my body needed. The apple and tomatoes from my pack up didn't help. I then opened a packet of crisps. I crunched the first salty disc without much hope; it was like magic! My taste buds came alive and I was immediately able to eat the rest of the packet, quickly followed by the rest of my lunch. What I hadn't realised was that my salt reserves must have been depleted by the sunny climb at the start of the day and by the extra effort needed to cope with being stranded in no man's land.

A spare packet of crisps has lived permanently in my rucksack since this incident and if I meet people who are feeling unwell after a steep climb, I usually suggest that, if a good slug of water doesn't help, they try taking on some salt. Many of us walkers are a healthy lot and probably don't have a high salt diet so when it comes to situations like these our bodies need an extra bit of help.

Incidentally, five minutes after leaving Seatallan, I was stripping back down to my shorts and t-shirt and making my way to Middle Fell and back to my waiting husband in the same summery conditions that I had set off in that morning. Peter had enjoyed a day sitting outside coffee shops and by the side of Wastwater, totally unaware that his wife had had anything other than an easy day's hike in perfect weather.

Apart from these memorable incidents, completing the Wainwrights didn't cause me too many problems. The very fact that the Wainwright Pictorial Guides are on sale in just about every shop in the Lake District and in the walking section of most book shops around Britain means that many of the fells are well known and often climbed. By choosing to walk during the week and in winter, I avoided the problem of the hoards queuing to cross Striding Edge or to reach the summit of Cat Bells that many peak baggers complain of. I had grown in confidence and was happy to challenge myself and as a result had some amazing experiences.

Chapter 11.
Two wonderful winter walks

Although the February walk in Ennerdale remains a highlight of The Wainwrights, there are two more winter outings that deserve a mention. On another February day in the final year of my challenge, I set out to bag Angle Tarn Pikes. The day was grey and very cold but the clouds were high. I drove to the secretive valley of Martindale. I climbed steeply up to the summit of Beda Head, realising that crampons would have been handy as the thin layer of frozen snow made walking difficult. I continued on the improving path, photographing icicles and incredible views as I went. As I gained altitude, I pulled my buff up around my chin against the biting cold. I was well padded and was protected by thermal undergarments but became aware that, although my body didn't feel too bad, the air I was breathing was becoming like ice. I pulled my buff higher. It was now covering my mouth and nose so that the air would be warmed by its fleece. As I reached Angle Tarn an unusual sight met my eyes; the tarn itself was frozen and covered with snow. The whole area, surrounded by white rocks, looked like a moonscape. There was no colour and it looked as though I had stepped into a monochrome photograph. I realised with a slight feeling of trepidation that if I was to slip here, I would become a victim of hypothermia long before any mountain rescue team could reach me.

After bagging the Pikes and taking some pictures of the scene, I decided to retrace my steps rather than risk going further. The walk was very eerie and as I descended towards the church in Howtown, I stopped to offer up a

Angle Tarn February 2010

prayer of thanks that I was safely back.

Only a few minutes later, I was reaching the magnificent summit cairn of Hallin Fell in bright winter sunshine with not a flake of snow on its grassy slopes. For me, this changing weather and landscape is one of the joys and mysteries of The Lake District but one that no-one must underestimate when they set off for an adventure on the fells.

A fortnight later, I was out in the snow again.

The walk to bag High Hartsop Dodd and Hartsop Above How, nearly had to be aborted, not due to poor weather but to stubborn bullocks and deep slurry. As I walked along the side of Brother's Water, conditions were perfect and I was looking forward to seeing the high fells covered in snow, under a blue sky. I reached the barn in front of my first ascent of the day. In the pen next to the barn were no less than nine bulls; not huge but still bulls. They weren't bothered by me and simply watched me with disdain as I tried to walk through the gate. I am sure they were amused as I quickly lifted my boot before it was engulfed by the thick brown liquid muck that covered the bottom of the pen in a layer over a foot deep. I decided that the only way to get around, was to edge my way along the metal fence with my backside towards the bemused herd. I went one way, only to find myself blocked by one obstinate animal that refused to move. I went back and tried the other way where the fence came to an end with a food trough filled with straw. This time I succeeded; climbing over the trough and dropping down safely into the field beyond.

The rest of the day was glorious. After the first steep climb, I found myself in virgin snow that gave easily beneath my boots. The snow reached my knees in places but the sunshine and the blue sky made the effort needed to walk in those conditions almost pleasurable. I would certainly rather be doing step-ups on the fells than in some cramped and sweaty gym. This was good for the soul. I walked on my own until Dove Crag where I met some walkers coming from the direction of Fairfield. We had a brief chat and took some photos before I settled down to have a well-earned lunch. I had more fun to come. My walk instructions talked about two steep descents. These could have been hard work but I chose to get down low and slide down the slopes using my poles as skis and when necessary, brakes. I made the summit of Hartsop above How just as the light was beginning to fade. A welcome pot of tea in the Kirkstone Inn, in front of a roaring fire made a perfect end to a perfect day in spite of its inauspicious start.

Chapter 12.
Completing the 214

By the summer of 2010, I was racing towards the end of my challenge.

At the end of May 2010, my husband volunteered to accompany a group of friends cycling from London to Paris for charity. He would drive the bikes to London and travel with them to their various checkpoints and campsites. He would be away for five days so I took the opportunity to book a bed and breakfast in Keswick with the intention of bagging as many of the remaining Northern Fells in those five days as I could.

I started by climbing High Rigg on the way to my digs just to warm up my legs and get me in the mood. I looked out over the wonderful mountain landscape laid out before me just waiting for my peak bagging frenzy. An old school friend was driving up to meet me in Keswick, with the intention of joining me on my walks for a couple of days. Karen had accompanied me on a couple of my previous walks, so thought she would enjoy a few days of serious hiking.

Our Bed and Breakfast was within walking distance of Keswick town centre so, after strolling down to gaze out over a tranquil Derwentwater, we had a lovely Indian meal and made our way back to look over the map at the next day's route and settle down for the night.

The day dawned bright and we set off to climb five Western Wainwrights starting with Burnbank Fell, which the great man himself describes as dull. However, as it was only the first of the day, I wasn't worried by this description. Our first obstacle was a field of cows which Karen found difficult to cross. At this stage, I hadn't had a problem with cows and wasn't too bothered by them. However, I was happy to take a detour, giving the cows a wide berth and we started our ascent, leaving the herd behind. Unfortunately, Karen, already feeling uncomfortable because of the cows, became aware of a niggling soreness at the back of her heel. Sure enough, she had got the beginnings of a blister. Looking at the steepness of the fell ahead of her and the distance I was planning to walk she didn't think that she would be able to join me. I was in a quandary. I enjoyed Karen's company and knew she was looking forward to the day but I had a challenge to complete and this was a chance to make good progress towards my goal.

I was very grateful when Karen offered to go back, which I thought was very generous considering the cows she would have to pass. We said our goodbyes and set off in opposite directions. I walked from Burnbank Fell to Blake Fell and then to Gavel Fell with no problems. I had no company on this hike, meeting only one other walker on Blake Fell who greeted me not with a cheery hello but with a question, 'Wainwrights or Nuttalls?'. I said I was doing the Wainwrights and he grunted, nodded and moved on. Whether he approved or not I was not sure.

The rest of the walk to Hen Comb and onto Mellbreak caused no real problems but was hard in the early summer heat. I was glad to be on my final fell of the day. What I hadn't reckoned on though was the horrible feeling of vertigo that I was to experience on the steep descent of Mellbreak, down to the Kirkstile Inn by Loweswater. I gingerly made my way down the steep face of the mountain looking at the patchwork of fields below which seemed to be undulating beneath me. I did reach the bottom safely but vowed never to use that route of descent ever again. Karen, who had had a lovely walk by Loweswater, met me with the words, 'You look like you've seen a ghost!' I think I would rather have faced one of those than the descent I had just completed. Still, I had another five summits ticked off. I began to relax and enjoyed a celebratory drink before heading back to Keswick for a meal, followed by a competitive game of scrabble and a good rest before starting out again the next day.

The next day I did a short walk up Ard Crags and Knott Rigg so that I could spend time with Karen visiting some of the spots we remembered from our school camp in Borrowdale. It was good to be sharing memories in the place we had camped, over forty years before.

Waking up to pouring rain the following morning, Karen decided to call it a day and went home after breakfast. I still wanted to do some walking so I decided to bag Walla Crag, an easy trek from the Bed and Breakfast. I walked along the shores of Derwentwater to reach Ashness Bridge, a beautiful, postcard perfect landmark, from where I made my ascent. By the time I was walking back to Keswick, raindrops were glistening on the summer flowers in the colourful gardens and the sun was taking over. I went back to my room to plan the rest of my day.

I made the decision to make an early evening ascent of Fellbarrow and Low Fell which proved a beautiful walk. It was a peaceful and, although I was alone, I was far from lonely. The morning rain had brightened the landscape. The yellow of the gorse and the white starry flowers on the Hawthorne stood out against the dark fells and the sparkling ripples on Loweswater. Little did I know that the peace of the Lake District was about to be shattered by an event so awful that no-one in their worst nightmares could ever have imagined occurring in this paradise.

Chapter 13.
A sad day for The Lake District

June 2nd 2010

For me, this was to be a great fell-bagging day and I started early, knowing that I would be heading back to Leeds before the day's end. For twelve others it would be the last day that they would enjoy the beauty of this wonderful world. It seems almost churlish to report on the peaks I bagged that day but while I was enjoying a great walk from Braithwaite, taking in the summits of Barrow, Outerside, Scar Crags, Sail and Causey Pike, I was wondering about the number of helicopters hovering around the area. I could hear other walkers commenting that the sunshine had probably encouraged people to push their limits and that The Mountain Rescue were having a busy day. How wrong they were.

I got down, feeling satisfied by the peaks I had bagged on my brief break and as I was pulling my boots off, for what I thought would be the last time that week, I was totting up my Wainwright total; one hundred and ninety-nine. I couldn't leave it there. I drove to Whinlatter Forest Park, as I decided I just had time to bag Brown How to make it a round two hundred, before coming down to the café there for a well-earned pot of tea.

It was on this particular summit that I met another hiker, who told me of the sad events that had taken place; A gunman, later named as Derrick Bird, had shot and killed twelve people and injured eleven more, before turning the gun on himself. My elation quickly turned to tears and disbelief. I walked slowly back to the Siskin's café and drank my tea in thoughtful dismay, watching the colourful birds chattering and tweeting in happy ignorance. I started my drive back to Leeds and pulled in to a lay-by to listen to the news. On hearing that one of the victims had been a lone walker, I started to worry about my husband hearing that news on his way back from Paris, knowing that his wife was in that area walking on her own. I did get a message to him via friends but had a sobering moment as I realised that it could have been me as I had been in the area of the shootings just twenty-four hours earlier.

We need to make sure that we make the most of every minute; life is precious.

Over the next couple of months, I made the most of every opportunity to drive up to The Lake District to 'mop up' the remaining fourteen fells.

One beautiful August day, I climbed up Lingcombe Edge from Buttermere, took a detour to climb Red Pike, (which surprisingly was shrouded in a light mist), just because it was there, before claiming the new summit of Starling Dodd. It was here that I met a lovely Cumbrian character with whom I got into conversation. He asked me where I was heading for and when I said Great Borne he shook his head and said in his wonderful accent, 'Eh Lass! Tha' doesn't want to do that. Farmer over t'other side shoots walkers.' I was a bit concerned to say the least. He went on to tell me that the land owner on the other side of Great Borne seemed to have a vendetta against hikers and dissuaded them from ascending this particular fell by erecting unwelcoming signs, removing stiles and constructing fences topped with trouser ripping barbed wire.

As I was set on the completion of my challenge, I decided to go ahead with my route to the top of Great Borne but to retrace my steps rather than descending by Floutern Tarn. I was so glad that I carried on, as the view from the summit was wonderful; yes, I did have to climb over a fence without the aid of a stile and I did leave the top pretty sharpish but it had been worth it. Retracing my steps proved to be a good move as I realised that I had dropped my map case earlier in the walk. On the descent back to Scales Force, I asked two lads on the way up the stepped footpath if they had seen it and sure enough, they had picked it up with the intention of asking any walkers they saw if it belonged to them. The map case wasn't a particularly good one and would soon need replacing anyway but I would have been sad to lose my trusty compass that had helped me out on so many occasions.

The last of my top fifty Wainwrights had been Lingmell. I was sure that I had reached its summit on that wet and windy spring day two years earlier. However, when I had been given a boxed set of Wainwright's Pictorial Guides for my fiftieth birthday, I perused the chapter on Lingmell. The pyramidal cairn that I had assumed marked the summit bore no resemblance to the cairn that Wainwright describes.

'Summit Cairns are welcome sights, but they are seldom objects of beauty or admiration. Here, however, on the highest point of Lingmell, is one of singular elegance, a graceful ten-foot spire that quite puts to shame the squat and inartistic edifice crowning the neighbouring very superior Scafell Pike.'

Lingmell had to be done again, or so I thought. The second ascent was as different as it could have been from the first. The weather was wonderful. I followed my original line; this time making a bee-line for the top unhampered by winds and driving rain. As I headed towards the towering structure described by the great man, I explored the surrounding area. I enjoyed looking at the precipitous crags and steep rocky slopes of the Northern and Eastern edges of the fell but my knees went to jelly and I felt a tingling in my toes when I realised that if I had strayed off course in the mist on that first ascent the day might have ended very badly. As I now know, the mound of stones that I had reached on the first occasion had indeed been the summit but the view of Great Gable from the graceful spire made the climb well worth the effort.

I got back to my car in good time and headed over to Hartsop to bag another peak before spending the night in the lovely Thorney How Youth Hostel, over thirty years after my first visit. As I walked into the beautiful Dovedale I came across an artist sitting by the river, peacefully drawing the fells. As my legs were already tired from my Lingmell climb, I did wonder, briefly, if perhaps I should take up a more peaceful hobby. The ascent to Middle Dodd was very steep and seemed to go on for ever but once on the top looking down to Brother's water and out to the many summits that I had climbed, I got a new lease of life and pressed on to climb Red Screes as its trig point was magnetically close.

I booked into Thorney How, knowing that the following day I would be climbing my penultimate Wainwright; Tarn Crag Easedale. I was so glad that I had chosen to stay at the home of the owl stamp once again, as I learnt that it was about to close as a YHA hostel and become independent. I bought a postcard, which I had stamped with the owl, before I left, and turned sadly from a place that held so many happy memories for me. I walked up Easedale, pondering what I had achieved. My legs seemed to know what was expected of them and I felt strong as I climbed above the tarn, over to Coledale Head and Sergeant Man. It was on this third fell that a gentleman asked me the way to Raise. I was so full of walking, that I offered not just to show him the way but to accompany him there.

On my way back to Grasmere, I decided to pay a second visit to Blea Rigg. It was here that I met a chap in his early eighties. He told me a story that gave me hope that, one day, a dream I had had as a ten-year-old might just come true. He and his wife, like me, had always wanted to settle in the Lake District. A couple of years earlier, they had driven back from a weekend in this incredible place and his wife had turned to him, in tears, saying that she didn't want to come again as leaving was getting too hard. They lived in a sheltered housing complex but were quite independent although her health wasn't good. A week after their visit to the Lakes, their housing complex acquired some computers and they signed up to learn how to use the internet. One of their first searches was for sheltered housing in The Lake District. They came across one and applied for a place. They couldn't believe it when they were accepted for a place and within a couple of months were fulfilling their dream. Tears filled my eyes as this wonderful man told me that he could now catch a bus and ramble in the fells above Ambleside and Grasmere, while his wife looks out over the hills and mountains, remembering the happy years they had both spent there. Dreams do come true.

I began to plan the celebrations for my final fell.

My daughters and some good friends were going to accompany me up Steel Fell in October. 10.10.10 would have been a nice neat date to finish on but as Saturday was more convenient for everybody, I would finish on the Ninth of October 2010. Peter was to drive us up the Easedale Road to wave us off and would be joining us for a celebratory meal in the evening. I was very proud of Hannah and Rebecca for their part in the day. Hannah enjoyed a country walk but was not fond of hills and Rebecca was coming over to The Lakes after working until the early hours of Saturday morning in the night club in Newcastle, where she was at university. There are several photographs of Rebecca sitting at the side of the path having a quick power nap and one of Hannah with a slightly hysterical smile on her face as she realised that the ascent of Helm Crag had to be done before we would be on the last leg back to Grasmere.

The steep grassy slope of Steel Fell or Dead Pike, (I think Hannah would think the latter was the more appropriate name), teased us with several false summits until finally, the cairn was in sight. I was encouraged to be the first to the summit, soon joined by the others. Rebecca pulled a bottle of champagne out of her rucksack together with a banner and a t-shirt that Peter had had printed for me. We shared our fizz and took a few pictures and I pushed a piece of paper into the cairn, on which I dedicated my achievement to my dad and to George who had fostered my love of The Lakes all those years ago. I had done it!

I wanted to record my fell bagging journey and started to write up all the Wainwrights in height order so that I could relive each one. I had fun recalling some amazing walks and putting photographs with the reports, to remind me of my adventures. I came to write up Whiteside and suddenly panicked. I had no photograph and couldn't remember when I had bagged this summit. I decided that I may have added it to The Coledale Round but I hated the feeling of uncertainty. One of the disadvantages of solo walking is that you have nobody to ask. I had to do it again. Even when I climbed this on a bright June day in 2012, I couldn't recall whether I had been there before or not. I took lots of pictures that day. Whiteside may indeed be my secret final fell.

Incidentally, my collection of Wainwright books has grown since my fiftieth birthday and I have been so pleased to be able to refer to Wainwright's summit diagrams which label the fells you can see from each summit. I am far from an expert but I am starting to recognise many of the peaks I have climbed, thanks to the great man. They have also helped me to find interesting routes up fells and avoid the masses who follow each other like sheep up the most popular paths.

Chapter 14.
Thoughts on walking solo

I enjoyed the feeling that I had completed the Wainwrights and that I had done it without too many mishaps. It was amusing though, to hear people's reactions to my achievement.

Many friends knew a little of what I was doing but were still surprised by the scale of it. However, the most common reaction was, 'Oh! You shouldn't walk on your own.', or 'Weren't you scared, being alone on the fells?' My answers were usually the same, 'I am rarely on my own in The Lake District.', and 'The fells of the Lake District are friendly mountains and you are not far from a village wherever you are.' If I hadn't chosen to walk solo, it would have taken a lot longer to complete my challenge but their comments did make me question what I had done and what I felt about being a lone hiker.

There is always a tummy turning moment when I throw my boots and rucksack in the car at some unearthly hour of the morning and set off on a new adventure. However, it is not long before I am singing and driving along with a tingle of excitement for the day ahead.

When you walk alone, you do need to plan carefully. You can't rely on anyone else for your food, water, maps or safety equipment

My route planning usually starts soon after I finish one walk so that I am ready for the next. I download a few of copies of my chosen route and tuck one copy into my rucksack with the OS map of the area. One copy is given to my husband, marked with any detours I might be tempted to take, one is put into my map case with my compass, (laminated if rain is expected) and a fourth will be put in the windscreen of my car. This last copy will have my husband's phone number and an ETA back at the car clearly visible, in the hope that someone, finding my car well after my ETA, might contact my husband or Mountain Rescue. This has never been used or needed but it has always seemed a sensible precaution to take.

Walking alone does mean that I have had to be prepared to carry a heavier pack than when walking with others. I carry a bivvy bag, spare clothes and food as well as plenty of water and a first aid kit. I also have a head torch with spare batteries.

I find that the start of a walk is often the most challenging part of the day. Often, if I start off on the wrong path, I can convince myself that I am on the right one for quite a while, so having no-one to check with, has occasionally meant a few false starts but once I'm on the path I can stride out looking forward to a good hike.

I walk at a steady pace which often increases once my legs have warmed up on my first ascent. I enjoy the fact that I can walk as quickly or as slowly as I like without having to match my pace with anyone else's. I don't often stop, except to enjoy the view, admire the flora or fauna or take photographs. I don't worry about how many people pass me or how many I pass although, if I am struggling, I will try to catch up with someone in front of me, just to increase my pace a little.

The benefits of my steady plodding were brought home to me on a walk over Helvellyn, soon after I had finished the Wainwrights. I had walked over Striding Edge to reach the summit of Helvellyn and felt full of walking. I wanted to walk over Nethermost and Dollywagon as I had only done these in a white-out so hadn't seen them properly. I bagged these summits and made my way down to Grisedale Tarn ready to climb St Sunday Crag. As I reached the tarn, I was approached by a younger walker who struck up a conversation. He looked at me quizzically and said, 'I have overtaken you three times, how come you are in front of me?' I wasn't quite sure how to answer other than to say that I had just carried on plodding and hadn't stopped very often. Anyway, we made our way over St Sunday Crag sharing walking tales, as hikers are apt to do. As we made our way down to the col, I went to take the path up to Birks and asked if he was joining me and he declined saying that he had nothing left in the tank and was heading down. I must admit to feeling pleased that I still had the stamina for a final fell and that my steady plodding had paid off.

People often ask me if I listen to music when I am walking. I can't imagine sticking headphones on and missing the sounds of nature. The sounds of the wind through the trees or a brook babbling down the hillside, the call of cuckoos in spring or just the perfect silence when you stand alone looking out at the fells around you, are sounds that make you feel alive.

Another common question is, 'What do you think about all day on your own?' The truth is, I have a rest from thinking. I am just concentrating on the terrain and my route and taking in my surroundings; from the majestic fells or a beautiful rainbow to a tiny patch of wild flowers beneath my feet. Walking alone probably means that I have seen more wildlife than those walking in large groups whose combined footsteps would frighten off a timid deer or perching peregrine. I can also stop to enjoy these sights for as long as I like without anyone to urge me to get moving.

Deer have become very special to me as I have walked the fells. I have lost count of the number of times that they have lifted my spirits when I have been plodding across seemingly featureless bog or just emerged out of thick mist. They have also shown me the way or reassured me that I am on the right track. Maybe this seems fanciful but I am happy to believe it, as their presence has been welcomed on too many occasions for it to be coincidence. Maybe, being herd animals, they sense a lone soul and feel the need to protect and look out for one that has gone astray from its own herd.

Having acquired a love of solo walking I had to decide on a new challenge.

I am sure that many Wainwright completers will share that, in the same breath that people are congratulating them, they are also likely to ask the question, 'What are you going to do next?'

Initially, I just decided that I was going to explore some hills closer to home. I had grown up in Lancashire and yet had never climbed Pendle Hill, so this was one I chose to climb a couple of weeks after Steel Fell. It is a lovely hill with great views and I have climbed it several times since. My daughter Hannah and her best friend decided to join me. As Hannah still wasn't keen on steep ascents, we took it steadily. There was no rush and the views as you look backwards on the steep steps to the summit are breath-taking. I was amused when, while having a brief stop, a chap looked at me assuming I was the one needing a rest. He patted my rucksack and said, 'You're doing very well love; not far to go now.' I smiled quietly to myself.

Chapter 15.
Aches and pains

Before I started my Wainwright challenge, I had been to my GP with concerns about a pain in my hip. It was intermittent and not chronic but when I felt it, I often had a feeling that my hip was giving way. I was told that it was probably bursitis which would be eased by taking Ibuprofen. I had returned several times over the years and been told the same thing. The pain had never got worse but even with all the walking I had done, my hip still didn't feel stable. Eventually, the doctor must have got fed up with me and decided that she would send me for some physiotherapy.

The physiotherapists were lovely and tried so many different ways to ease the pain in my hip that they became puzzled. They decided that they would give me steroid injections, guided by ultrasound, into the site of the pain. I prepared for this but on the day, I was surprised by the findings, as was the senior physiotherapist; there was no bursitis. I asked to see a different doctor at the practice to discuss this, who immediately sent me for an MRI scan. It turned out that I had a disc bulge and that there were several areas of minor to moderate degeneration in my spine. The disc bulge on the right- hand side of my spine had been encroaching on my nerve root. I finally had an explanation for the pain I had been experiencing for about five years. The physiotherapists now had something to work with and I was given exercises to ease the disc bulge by stretching my spine. And the localised pain in my hip was helped by acupuncture in the same department.

I finally felt that my hip pain had been sorted once and

for all and I was ready for something new without the worry that my hip would give way while I was walking. My advice to someone suffering any pain is not to accept the usual explanation that it is 'just your age' but to ask for a proper explanation and treatment if necessary.

Chapter 16.
The next challenge

I had discovered some great little fells and excellent walks within an hour of home but I soon began itching for more. It wasn't long before I decided that I was going to do Wainwright's Coast to Coast Walk. I had done The Dale's Way solo in 2007 and had enjoyed it so this seemed the next logical step.

I started to plan for my next challenge. I tried to make my walks longer and I chose to walk in all weathers so that I would be prepared for anything that might be thrown at me during the two weeks that it would take to walk the one hundred and ninety- two miles from St Bees on the West Coast to Robin Hood's Bay on the East coast of Northern England.

I went back to the Lake District several times, doing some of my favourite horseshoes again, and climbed several Yorkshire Peaks while searching websites and reading up on the walk..

One wet April day. I sat at the computer with a list of phone numbers of Youth Hostels and Bed and Breakfast Accommodation. I phoned them in order, booking provisionally, as the stops had to be carefully worked out with the distances between them. By the end of the day, I had confirmed my bookings. My tummy was doing somersaults; I had taken on another challenge.

I continued my training, which went well and I felt my fitness improving as I increased the miles that I was walking. There were a couple of memorable incidents during the following months, one of which nearly stopped my walk before I had taken the first step.

The first incident, which proved an interesting battle with the elements, took place on a fine spring day in The Lake District. The forecast was for clear bright weather with a light breeze. Peter drove me to Ambleside and I set off with the intention of walking The Fairfield Horseshoe, a familiar route, which I had decided would be a good training ground. I walked towards Rydal looking forward to the day ahead. There was indeed a gentle breeze but it was quite pleasant. However, as I started the steep climb up Nab Scar, it quickly became gustier. As I reached the ladder stile giving onto the open fell, I had to wait for over a dozen people all coming the other way. It was too early in the day for them to be returning from an anti-clockwise circuit of the horseshoe so I was puzzled. I soon learnt that conditions on the fell were very different to those on the low-level trek to Rydal.

I was advised by several of the walkers that passed me to turn back as the wind was too strong to go on.

I am not fool-hardy but knew that there would be a possibility that I would meet strong winds on The Coast to Coast so here was a chance to test my ability to cope in such conditions. I pushed on; head down, doing battle with sudden gusts that threatened to take me off my feet. My improved fitness meant that I made quite good progress over Heron Pike and I headed to Great Rigg. At this point, if I stopped moving, I was blown backwards and indeed I did turn and allow the wind to take me back a few metres so that I could take breather and then carry on. As I approached the final climb to Great Rigg, I met two fairly rugged male walkers who were lying down on the waving grass at the side of the path. They propped themselves up as I approached and told me that they had had enough and needed a break from the battering they were taking from the now gale force wind.

I made a decision at the point that I would reach Great Rigg summit and then head down over Stone Arthur. I felt pleased that I had got as far as I had and that I was able to make a plan for an onward walk rather than just allowing myself to give up at the first hurdle.

When I got back to Ambleside and met Peter for a well-earned cuppa, I found out that someone had told him that it was a 'bit breezy' on the fells. I guessed that this was a walker with a talent for understatement or one that hadn't gone further than Nab Scar. Still, it had been good training.

Another incident on a training walk had more serious consequences and had me questioning whether the walk would still be possible.

Less than a month before my walk, a friend from work, another Karen, fancied climbing Ingleborough one of the Yorkshire Three Peaks. The weather wasn't brilliant; a bit drizzly after an incredibly dry April but, as I had to get the miles in, I was more than happy to go. We made good time up the clear paths from Clapham to reach the wonderful pot hole of Gaping Gill. Having spent a minute or two looking at this magnificent sight, Karen started to cross the river. I made a move towards the bridge saying, 'I'm going round I don't do rivers.' This wasn't totally accurate but, on the whole, I prefer to walk a few hundred yards and use a bridge as the chances of slipping and twisting or breaking something while crossing a river are fairly high, not to mention that you are likely to get wet feet; not the most comfortable for walking.

Karen continued across, saying, 'Look, it's dry here, you'll be fine.' Against my better judgement, I followed her and of course my feet found a patch of wet limestone and flew out from under me. I had visions of being carried by the water down the huge cavern that we had been admiring only moments earlier so I planted my hand down firmly, to hold myself still. A pain shot up my arm as I started to get to my feet. My friend asked if I was okay and I replied, 'I'm fine but I've broken my thumb.' This was said half in jest and as she came to help me and slipped herself, we were both laughing; with only a touch of hysteria. As she was already crouching down, Karen didn't hurt anything other than her pride. Once we were safely on the ongoing path, we assessed our injuries. She had nothing worse than a wet bottom and I said my thumb was sore but that I felt fine to go on. We continued on our way to the summit of Ingleborough without incident. It was a bit windy and drizzly on top so we didn't stay around long and we were soon on our way down. My thumb hadn't given me much trouble except when trying to unzip a pocket on my rucksack. However, when we got to the car, I removed my gloves and the size and colour of the joint at the bottom of my painful digit told me that I had done more damage than I initially thought

Luckily, I wasn't driving and the decision was made to call in at Airedale A and E on the way home. My friend left me in the safe hands of the nursing staff. I was seen, assessed, and given an X-ray which was inconclusive. I was given a temporary splint and Karen picked me up and returned me to my own car which I drove gingerly home.

I had been told to go to the fracture clinic in Leeds a few days later. When I did this, I was given another x-ray which this time showed a broken scaphoid bone. As I was being fitted with a bright pink pot and wondering about how it would affect my Coast-to-Coast Plans, I spoke to the doctor doing the job. He was so understanding and said that If I came back to him a few days before my walk, he would make sure that the plaster was comfortable and fitted with the walking poles I would be using. How wonderful is our NHS?

Chapter 17.
The Coast to Coast

Only four weeks later, with my arm safely encased in its new pot, Peter drove me to St. Bees, on the West Coast, where we stayed in a B&B, ready for me to start the walk the next morning. Peter and I went down to the beach before we turned in for the night so that I could dip my toe in the Irish Sea and choose a pebble to carry to Robin Hood's Bay. As I bent down to pick up my chosen stone, my phone dropped from its case into the water beneath my feet. I wasn't too concerned but I guess a lot of my friends would have been horrified. A constant refrain, from people wishing me well for my walk the previous week, had been, 'Make sure you keep your mobile phone well charged!' Oops! Even before I had started, I had rendered my phone useless. I knew that it was unlikely that I would have had coverage for much of the Lake District section of the walk but it wasn't ideal. Still, I remained hopeful that it would dry out over the

On Dent Fell, May 2011

next couple of days.

In spite of the fact that it was the end of May, I woke on the first day of my adventure to cold wind and rain.

I had butterflies, the size of elephants, doing a dance in my stomach, but I got kitted up in full wet weather gear and waved goodbye to Peter and some friends from Leeds who were staying in the area and had come to see me on my way. Pushing against the wind and watching the huge waves lashing the cliffs I did wonder whether I was totally mad. As Wainwright says, it is a bit disconcerting to be walking West but he encourages the walker to enjoy the delights of Fleswick Bay; even that wasn't exactly welcoming on this particular day and my spirits only really lifted when I finally started to walk inland toward The Lake District Hills.

Just before I climbed my first peak of the walk; Dent Hill, the rain stopped and the sun began pushing through the clouds. As usual, climbing a hill lifted my mood and I felt great as I reached the summit and was able to look down towards the beautifully named Nanny Catch, my gateway to the Lakes, and ahead towards the glorious mountains which seemed to be drawing me in. Two other Coast to Coasters joined me at the large cairn and I was able to get them to take a photograph of me at the summit.

When I reached Ennerdale without any problem, I began to feel that I wasn't quite so mad after all.

I hadn't been able to book a B&B in Ennerdale itself so, after having a drink and chatting with a small group of fellow walkers, I used the hotel phone to contact my hosts who picked me up and took me back to their lovely home where I was fed and watered. I was quite tired so went to bed fairly early for me and, after a quick read, fell into a deep sleep. I awoke feeling refreshed thinking that it was morning. I took a look at my clock as it still seemed quite dark; it was two o'clock in the morning. Try as I might, I couldn't get back to sleep. I read, I had a drink, I snuggled down, drifted for maybe fifteen to twenty minutes and woke up again. I was glad when breakfast time arrived and I could start my day properly.

I was a bit worried about my lack of sleep but decided that it was probably just first day adrenalin that had set my mind racing and that after the fourteen miles to Borrowdale, I would make up for it the next night.

Although the heavy rain stopped me walking over Angler's Crag or doing the High Stile alternative, both suggested as exciting routes by Wainwright, I had a lovely day. I enjoyed visiting Black Sail Youth Hostel for the first time in over thirty years. The kindly warden had put a large urn of boiling water on a table ready for passing walkers to make themselves a hot drink because of the bad weather. Unfortunately, although there was a notice saying that we could help ourselves to a drink, there was a second notice politely asking that we refrain from using the toilets. Without a chance to visit the loo, I decided I couldn't avail myself of the tea or coffee on offer. Again, the weather cleared by midday and the climb up Loft Beck onto Moses Trod made me realise that my training was paying off. I loved every minute of it and didn't seem to be huffing and puffing too badly on the steep ascent.

I reached a little cottage in Rosthwaite and was shown to my room. I was pleased to see a bath in the bathroom as I fancied a soak in the tub, hoping that it might contribute to a more settled night's sleep. Unfortunately, though there was a bath, a plug was conspicuous by its absence and I had to settle for a shower. Presumably, not allowing guests to use too much water helped to keep the costs down for the owner of this particular establishment.

After a shower and change, I walked down to the Langstrath Inn where I replenished my calories with a welcome bowl of pasta.

Fourteen miles of walking plus extra to the Inn and back and a good meal inside me, I was bound to sleep that night. Well, that was the hope. As with the previous night, I slept deeply from ten thirty until the early hours of the morning and from then on, not a wink.

This pattern was repeated the following night when I was staying at Patterdale Youth hostel. There had been another sixteen miles or so of glorious walking, climbing out of Borrowdale, over Lining Crag and descending into Grasmere before climbing again out of that valley on a familiar route to Grisedale Tarn and from there down into Patterdale. The day was beautiful with only a little light rain for an hour or two at its start. It was a long walk but, walking over countryside that I knew well, the miles passed easily. In fact, I felt so full of walking that I began to wish I had walked over St Sunday Crag but on the long route into Patterdale I was surrounded by beautiful views, verdant pastures and very endearing calves, and lambs gambolling happily in the sunshine. I also had the joy of knowing that I was going to be well fed that night in the company of good friends. Our Vicar from Leeds, Jonathan Clark, was staying in a holiday home at the far end of Ullswater with his family. He picked me up from the hostel soon after I arrived there, and took me to their accommodation for the evening.

Fluffy towels and luxurious bubble bath had been left in the bathroom where I finally had the long soak that I had been craving. Jonathan's wife Mary, a GP, was determined that I would have a good night's sleep that night. After my bath, she fed me well with pork, from a joint which had been cooking slowly in the Aga all day, accompanied by fresh vegetables, and roast potatoes as white and as fluffy inside as the towels. She then ensured that the coffee I drank was decaffeinated, before she delivered me back to the hostel and my bed for the night.

In spite of being in a very busy dorm on a not so comfortable bottom bunk, I fell asleep pretty quickly. Incidentally, I had not expected a featureless, rather uninviting dormitory at Patterdale. When I had hostelled in the 1970s and 80s, Patterdale was categorised as a 'special' hostel. I know, if I had a choice now between the basic Black Sail and special Patterdale hostel, which one I would choose.

As on the previous two nights, I awoke at 2:00am. This time though I couldn't even turn my light on to read or make myself a comforting cup of tea. After a trip to the loo, I climbed back into bed, trying not to disturb anyone else. I lay as still as I could, looking at the slats of the bunk above me, listening to gentle snores and heavy breathing all around me. I was not going to get to sleep like this so after an hour I grabbed my fleece and tiptoed out, book in hand and stayed in the cold members' lounge reading until I felt tired enough to try again. I may have drifted off when I eventually went back to bed at about 04:30 but I certainly didn't feel particularly ready for the day ahead when I trudged in for a canteen style breakfast at 08:00 after a rather measly shower in a non- too clean cubicle. How I was managing this walk on about four and a half hours sleep a night, I didn't know. I wasn't only managing the walk; I was actively loving every minute of the Coast-to -Coast so far.

The day ahead was one that I was really looking forward to as I was to reach the highest point of the route; the summit of Kidsty Pike.

I set off from the Youth Hostel in relatively clear weather with my waterproof packed away for once.

I knew the path up to Boredale Hause well, as I had used it when climbing Place Fell only a few months before. As I reached the hause, the mist started to close in a bit. A group of three Coast-to -Coast walkers trotted to catch up with me to ask if I knew where I was going. When I replied in the affirmative, they asked if they could join me as they weren't sure of the route. We then caught up with another couple who were studying their map and who joined the party. The six of us made our way past Angle Tarn as the cloud closed in. It got cool enough for me to don my gloves and a hat but I couldn't be bothered taking my pack off to get my coat out as I was only slightly damp and I don't like walking in too many layers if I can help it.

We walked together and as a figure loomed up out of the mist descending from Kidsty Pike on his way to Patterdale we chatted and he pointed out our onward path without any need for us to consult our maps or guide books.

I still feel that I was cheating at this point. Would I have found the path had I been on my own? I am sure I would, but being an independent minded soul who was determined to navigate the route for myself, I still feel that one day I ought to do that part of the walk again without assistance. Silly I know; but some of you reading this will understand.

At the summit of Kidsty Pike, I finally donned my coat as I knew I would feel colder going down without the effort of the ascent to keep me warm. As I did so the other walkers started clapping which I thought very odd. Apparently, they had been trying to guess when I would finally give in to the cold and put my outer layer on. We laughed and set off for the descent to Haweswater. As we did so, we descended out of the cloud and our way became clear. There was now no need to stay as one group so we took photographs for each other, said our goodbyes and made our way down at our own speed. I walked fairly slowly at this point as the descent required a bit of scrambling which was difficult with only one useful arm. I enjoyed the challenge and felt quite pleased with myself when I began the long but beautiful walk to the far end of the lake on a path coloured with bright yellow gorse and hawthorn trees in their rose white blossom, accompanied by beautiful bird song. Although the earlier company had been welcome, I was glad to be walking alone again.

I was staying just at the end of the lake in Bampton Grange, a mile off the official route but which had a lovely looking inn called The Crown and Mitre where, for the first day since Sunday, I was going to spend the night with my husband. I was shown to our room and was stunned by its whiteness. I was mucky with the sweat and the healthy dirt of a day's walking. I was very careful not to sit down anywhere until I had showered and changed. Peter arrived and we treated ourselves to a wonderful meal of slow braised lamb shank known as Lamb Henry which is probably our favourite Cumbrian meal. It was lovely to catch up and to relax in luxury. When I snuggled down that night with a familiar arm around me, I fell into the deepest sleep so far and I didn't wake up until the birds started singing at about 6:30. I had slept all night! Bliss!

I waved goodbye to my husband the next morning with a spring in my step and the sun in the sky. I felt replenished by the good meal, a fantastic night's sleep and the love of my husband sending me on my way. I was walking to Orton which, at eleven miles without the ascents of the previous days would be a fairly gentle stroll. This gave me time to explore the remains of Shap Abbey which I was very happy to do. The ruins are worth a visit and speak of a time when life was slower and as Wainwright notes,' buildings had grace and dignity and beauty because they were built in such peaceful surroundings'. It was lovely to spend time feeling the peace of years surround me as I wandered about the ruins before pushing on towards Orton.

Chapter18.
Goodbye to Lakeland

Soon after leaving Shap, the route of the Coast-to-Coast crosses over the busyness of cars whizzing up and down the M6. I felt enormously grateful that I had over a week before I had to join the rat race again.

I noted very soon after crossing the motorway that I could see outcrops of limestone which were very striking after the hard granite that I had been walking on for several days, I was saying goodbye to the Lake District. I looked back for my last glimpse at the wonderfully familiar fells and the summit of Kidsty Pike that I had climbed only the previous day but which looked miles away

Wainwright's words about this point on the trail almost make you think that the rest of the walk isn't worth doing.

'This is farewell to Lakeland, and farewells to Lakeland are always sad. What follows is anti-climax—level walking instead of up and down, trees and fields and villages instead of rough and lonely hills; lovely, yes, but not exceedingly beautiful as the crossing of Lakeland has been. Well, it's not too late to abandon the coast-to-coast idea and stay on in Patterdale. There is nothing as good ahead.'

I was enjoying this experience far too much to give up now. As I walked away from the Lake District, I did feel some of the nerves returning. For the last three days I had been on very familiar territory with little fear of losing my way. I had been walking in those friendly hills for over forty years and now I was leaving my friends and going into the unknown.

As if to say their own goodbye, there were huge erratic boulders from the West, strewn across the new limestone landscape, left there by the ice age as if to impose themselves on the softer and gentler terrain as a reminder of their greatness.

One sight that brought a smile to my face and a lightness to my step was the increasing number of wild flowers. Narrow paths, bordered by waving cow parsley, ragged robin, meadow cranesbill and bright buttercups, made my exit from the first part of the walk a colourful and attractive one.

The history that I had felt at Shap Abbey was overtaken by a simpler but much older sight; The Oddendale Stone Circle. Some may not find it the most exciting of landmarks but stone circles give me a sense that I was following paths made by footsteps of Ancient Britons who once peopled the landscape.

I walked on, lunching on a hill near a large quarry. I didn't think that I was in quite the right place but knew I couldn't be far off the route. I had decided that by climbing to a vantage point I might be able to see where I should be going. Indeed, after consulting my instructions and looking down to landscape below, I spotted the step stile that marked my onward route. On reaching Orton, I was greeted not by other walkers or welcoming locals but by numerous scarecrows in various guises dotted about the village including one in a nightdress being rescued by Fireman Sam from an upstairs window of my accommodation for the night.

The owner was very welcoming, but less welcome was the information that the pub was no longer serving meals. However, this enterprising lady had worked out a solution for her hungry guests. I was given a menu from Tebay services on the M6. Having chosen a tasty sounding meal, I went to have another luxurious bath in a well-appointed Victorian styled bathroom. By the time I was changed, my meal had been collected and was waiting in her warm oven ready to be decanted from its foil containers onto willow pattern plates. Although I was left to eat alone, my meal was very pleasant and as good as any pub grub would have been.

Rather than stay in the B&B alone, I decided to have a walk round the pretty village and have a look at some more of the scarecrows. The church in Orton is very pretty. As I approached, I noticed that it looked surprisingly busy for a Thursday. I then realised that it was Ascension Day. I decided to join the congregation and enjoyed a lovely evening in their company. While returning to my digs after the service, I decided to try turning my phone on; something I had tried every day to no avail. I was amazed when it suddenly sprung into life as though there had never been anything wrong.

I had no trouble sleeping which was a relief and when

I woke I felt amazing; it was almost as though this was the first day of the walk. I walked out of the village on the hottest day of the trek so far.

I had looked forward to sunshine but by the end of the day, I was thinking,' be careful what you wish for'. I wasn't doing any climbing so wouldn't be able to enjoy the cool breeze of a mountain summit. The walk began along a bridleway with another stone circle; Gamelands Stone Circle, just over the wall alongside the path. After stopping to take a photograph, I made my way over a series of pastures, the route here was easy underfoot but it offered no shade from the baking heat. I was looking forward to reaching Sunbiggin Tarn hoping that there would be a cool bank to rest on where I could perhaps dangle my hands, and maybe my feet into its refreshing water. However, on reaching the tarn, I became aware that it would offer no respite. An area of special scientific interest, it is surrounded by a tangle of heather and apparently is often crowded with the clamour of breeding gulls. As I approached the tarn alone, I could hear nothing; no crying gulls, no gently lapping water. The tarn was low, empty of birds and had no gently sloping bank on which to spend a pleasant five minutes. I walked away from the tarn that I had looked forward to reaching without a backward glance.

At this point, I became aware of my broken arm which had not bothered me too much since setting off from St Bees. It was beginning to feel as though it was roasting inside my plaster. I was wearing a buff to protect my neck from the strong sun but after slapping a thick layer of sun-cream on every exposed inch of skin, I took my buff and placed it over my plaster hoping that it might reflect more heat than the pink fibreglass cast which seemed to be absorbing every ray. It didn't really make any difference and my bandanna was swapped from neck to arm and back as I walked, being used most effectively as a fan as I wafted it in front of my face moving it from one to the other. I began to follow a wall down into Smardale and noticed that the sheep were obviously struggling with the heat too. They were wandering lazily from one part of the wall to another, hunkering down in its narrow shadow. The sun was high in the sky so there was no hope of a shadow wide enough for me to hunker down in, so I pressed on. This should have been an easy, delightful day's walking but I was too worried about running out of water, getting sunstroke, or roasting like an overdone piece of beef, to enjoy it as much as I had expected too.

Smardale Bridge and the surrounding area is really pretty and I was able, momentarily, to appreciate my surroundings, stopping to take a picture of a lively skylark that seemed to accompany me for a while; twittering excitedly overhead and landing on the wall in front of me. Maybe it was just making sure that I wasn't going to disturb its nest but it was a welcome distraction and made me smile. I was enjoying one of the benefits of being a lone walker as I guess a bird like this would be unlikely to approach a large group or maybe walkers in a large group would be unlikely to notice a noisy skylark above their chatter. As I reached the beck, pretty wild flowers added colour to the scene; the pink of the Herb Robert standing out against the grass which was yellowing in the sun. On the gentle climb over Smardale Fell, I started to hear a sound which I had feared for the last few miles, I was starting to suck air as well as water from my reservoir. Luckily, the route ran largely down-hill to Kirkby Stephen from that point but I hate running out of water. This is not something I have done very often but it is not a pleasant experience. It is amazing how thirsty you feel when you know that drinking is no longer a possibility. The horses and sheep seemed to watching me as I approached the tunnel marking the entry into the town as if to say, 'These silly humans; what are they doing walking miles in this heat'.

I almost staggered into the first pub I got to; asking for a lime and soda with lots of ice and a pint of water. A bottle of Bollinger Champagne could not have tasted any better than that glass of Adam's Ale. My thirst quenched, I was relieved to realise that I hadn't roasted and that I still felt well, without the dizziness and muddled thinking that would have indicated sunstroke. After a packet of salted peanuts to replenish my lost sodium, I was amazed to feel ready to make my way to the Youth Hostel without any side effects resulting from a day's walking under the hot sun; mind you the day had given me no desire to try a desert trek.

Though the Youth Hostel in Kirkby Stephen is a private hostel, it had a lovely friendly atmosphere and now that I was sleeping well, I was looking forward to the camaraderie. The dormitory that I was allocated was a small room with only one bunk. My room-mate soon arrived; another lone walker who was exploring the country having recently moved from America. We shared our stories and went for showers emerging feeling clean, tired and very hungry. We decided that the pub, more or less next door to the hostel, would be the best place to eat. It was good to be eating in company; I never mind walking alone but eating on my own isn't as pleasurable. We made our way back to the hostel and started planning for the next day.

Because of my broken arm, I had made the decision to use a packhorse service to carry my luggage from place to place. This meant that I only had to carry a day sack. After checking the weather forecast, packing for the following day and checking my onward route I settled down for a good night's sleep. I was pleased that Melissa, my room-mate, was happy to turn in for the night at the same time.

Chapter 19.
Company, peat bogs and bird song

I awoke the next morning to another sunny day. Melissa was up and off before I had finished my breakfast. This was going to be the only day of my adventure that I was going to have company for the whole of the day. My friend, Jenny, was coming over from Leeds and, after dropping her off at the hostel, her husband was going to drive to Appleby where he would enjoy the delights of the annual horse fair for the day, before meeting us again in Keld. By the time Jenny arrived, the sun was starting to hide itself behind the occasional cloud but with a bit of a breeze, it was promising to be a pleasant day for walking. The route from Kirkby Stephen to Keld could have been difficult in mist as it goes over boggy, peaty ground at Nine Standards Rigg so Jenny and I were glad of the clear conditions.

We made our way through the picture-perfect hamlet of Hartley, stopping on route to chat to a friend of Jenny's who happened to be pottering in her garden, much to Jenny's delight. It was lovely to be sharing the day with a friend who is such easy company. We have walked together several times and seem to match our pace and our rest stops without trying. We also share a love of birds, flowers, glorious views and waterfalls; in fact, any of the wild and wonderful features that make a walk so worthwhile. I stopped for Jenny to take my picture at the signpost to Nine Standard Rigg and as I did so I heard a sweet high chirruping close to my right boot. I looked down into the tufty grass to spot three beautiful grouse chicks being hurried on their way by a harassed looking female determined to get them away from the large boots which threatened their survival if they strayed too close to the well- trodden path.

As we made our way to the watershed, the wind started to get stronger and the clouds thickened so that the nine stone pillars that marked the summit were coming and going from our view. By the time we reached them, the day bore no resemblance to the one we had set off in. We had donned our waterproofs and were holding onto our hoods as the wind whipped the drizzle into our faces.

I was looking forward to the views described by Wainwright; Westward views into Lakeland and over to the North, the massifs of Cross Fell and Mickle Fell, two fells whose acquaintance I was still to make. To the South, I was hoping to see the hills of Mallerstrang and the beautiful valley of Swaledale. What could I see? Strange cairns looking like giants in the mist and a variety of colourful blobs, belonging to bright cagoule clad walkers, hopping and leaping across the very boggy ground. Jenny and I felt very lucky to have happened upon this large group of Coast-to-Coasters at this point.

Not only did it mean that we had help with route finding but by watching which walkers made it from one patch of relatively dry peat to another without sinking we could pick our way across without losing our boots in depths that had claimed several walking poles which we could see poking through the dark mud; we hoped these hadn't been attached to people who had sunk without trace.

The drizzle had turned to heavy rain and the wind wasn't giving us much respite from the battering we were taking. According to Wainwright, 'The attainment of Nine Standards Rigg is an occasion for celebration.' Jenny and I were celebrating getting across the worst of the bog but didn't stop around to mark this in any way. The party ahead of us made very sensibly for a corrugated iron bothy. We joined them and spent a sociable quarter of an hour or so, protected from the weather, eating our snacks and sharing stories of the walk so far.

As we emerged from the hut, the clouds started to thin out and the sun bravely made its way through the grey sky and brightened our path to the inviting cluster of farm buildings that is Ravenseat, where we were hoping to wet our whistles with a pot of tea and taste Amanda Owens' famous scones. Our luck was out though as the chalk board propped against the bridge informed us that there would be no refreshments that day. This made us very glad that we had spent time eating our crisps and fruit in the hut. The scene was still a rural idyll after the blackness of the peat. The yellow aconites, decorating the stones at the edges of the river, were sparking brightly after being washed by the recent rain.

Our waterproofs came off and we were able to enjoy the rest of the walk towards Keld without incident. This part of the route has some wonderful scenery with several waterfalls pouring over chalky white limestone into the River Swale. However, as we approached Keld, it wasn't the sights that attracted our attention as much as the increased swell of birdsong. We had heard the young grouse at the start of the day but the bleak moorland had been silent on the whole, apart from the whistle of the wind in our ears. All of a sudden there were so many birds that they seemed to be competing for the prize of being the loudest or doing the best arial display. In a mile or so we saw and heard dozens of lapwings, curlews and oyster catchers. I daresay, if we hadn't been looking skyward, we would have seen dippers on the river and swifts, swooping low and making the most of the insects swarming in the damp air. A celebratory fanfare of trumpets couldn't have given us a better welcome into the small hamlet of Keld.

We met up with Jenny's husband, Ian, who had had a wonderful day at The Appleby Fair, and made our way to a little shop which served hot drinks and home-made cake. We all opted for a lovely mug of hot chocolate, over which we shared our stories of the day. Jenny and Ian then saw me to my digs before setting off to drive back to Leeds. It was strange to think that it would be over a week until I was going to be heading back there while they would be home in only a couple of hours.

I was staying at Butt House which was a pleasant, efficiently run establishment and meals were served at the nearby Keld Lodge, run by the same proprietors.

In spite of eating a lovely piece of salmon with fresh vegetables for my dinner I was actually craving a meal that was cheaper and tastier; such as a good spaghetti bolognaise or lasagne. I found that other than the meal I had had at the Langstrath Inn in Borrowdale; restaurants catering for those walking the Coast to Coast, seemed to think that all walkers want a meat (or fish) and two veg. meal for which they could be charged the earth. The simple bar meals of pie and chips, chilli and rice or pasta and sauce seemed sadly absent. Although I could make no complaints about the meal or the accommodation, I was surprised that there seemed to be a lack of cosiness or camaraderie somehow. At breakfast, rather than being served by a friendly host bearing large pots of tea and plates of hot buttery toast, the items of food were wheeled in on heated hostess trolleys for guests to help themselves. Maybe it was because I had had lovely company on the previous day but something of the chatter and bustle of the earlier part of the walk were missing and I was quite glad when I was ready to leave and start walking even though the rain and mist had returned.

I had intended to explore the high- level route, through long abandoned lead mines, from Keld to my next stop in Reeth. However, it quickly became apparent that this would not be sensible. I was pondering this as I met up with a Pennine Way walker; a reminder that, here the route running North to South crosses the Coast-to- Coast going West to East. We chatted for a while, discussing the merits of the two trails and by the time we parted, I had been caught by a couple of other walkers going to Reeth. They too had been debating which route they would use to get there. I walked along with them, admiring the beautiful waterfalls and the ruins of Crackpot Hall, at which point the track to the mines leaves the more direct one following the banks of The River Swale. We compared our various walk books. My Cicerone Guide promised a spectacular display of wild flowers and lush meadow; 'riparian loveliness at its best', if we were to stay on the Right Royal Road to Reeth while Wainwright,

next section of
ound particularly

al scenery and have an
t enjoy this section of the
e is for high ground and rough
us.'

efers to Danby Wiske, a small hamlet
d at the lowest altitude of the walk and
I was staying for the night as, 'The slough
; not exactly encouraging.

ever, it was a beautiful day and I decided to make
most of whatever it was to bring. With my
xpectations low, my spirits were immediately lifted by the sight of the River Swale sparkling in the sunlight and the easy walking under my feet. I was also heartened by the large number of direction signposts. These weren't always the usual finger posts or footpath signs but took the form of yellow arrows painted on wooden gates and stiles or more interestingly, yellow frisbees nailed to trees which I could spot across fields of well-ordered crops. I was fascinated by all the different greens in the plants around me, comparing them in my head to my embroidery threads neatly stowed in my sewing box back home. However, not having a clue about farming, I couldn't identify any of them.

It was while I was walking through one of these fields

though dedicating several pages to describing and drawing the mines of Swinner Gill and Gunnerside does say that there is little beauty in this direction and suggests that if the day be wet or misty the low- level route is the way to go. I had noticed that the wild flowers seemed to be at their best and walking into the mist onto abandoned mining track held little appeal so I chose to walk beside the river.

It was a good choice. The glorious Yorkshire Dales meadows were at the peak of their beauty. Although the day stayed fairly damp, the rain wasn't cold and with the sun that kept peeping through the clouds, it made the grass greener and flowers brighter than they would have been on a dry dusty day. There was one heart-stopping moment in the day when; as I approached Reeth the simple narrow path that I was walking along changed, disconcertingly, into a wall high above the river. The rain had made the wall rather slippery and I made my way rather tentatively along this section before it became an innocuous path by the river once again. This had probably been the easiest day's walking so far; twelve miles with no major ascents and I was feeling good especially knowing that I had passed the half way mark. I was also going to be able to spend another evening celebrating with friends and with my husband again. The Reverend Caroline Hewlett who had been a curate at our church in Leeds was, by 2011, Vicar of four churches in Swaledale and Arkengarthdale.

The vicarage where she lived with her husband, was situated along The Coast-to-Coast Route; though as I write this, it has had to be moved, as the house I stayed in was subject to serious flooding on two occasions. Caroline and her husband had invited me to stay when they knew I

was doing the walk, which was lovely. However, it was only at a later date that they had suggested Peter come up to join me there. We had already booked a night t
at my next stop in Richmond so I was going t
company for two evenings which was really spe
almost felt like cheating to be so spoilt.

After a sociable evening and restful sleep, I was a
set off quite leisurely the next morning after a breakf
home-made savoury muffins knowing that I only ha
and a half miles of pleasant Dales paths to wal
Richmond.

For lovers of England's 'green and pleasant land',
walk from Reeth to Richmond is a sheer delight. For r
although I do love the Dales, I still prefer the rugg
heights of the high peaks of the Lake District. Howev
this didn't detract from the beautiful scenery that this da
afforded in bucket loads As I made my way acros
Grinton Bridge the route became familiar as I approache
Marrick Priory. A few years earlier, Peter, the girls and I had enjoyed a fun weekend there with a church group from Leeds. I smiled as I remembered my husband wriggling his 6' 5' frame through a narrow pipe as part of a pot holing experience during our time there and the girls laughing excitedly while trying out the ropes' course. Something else that was a clear memory from that previous visit was the number of rabbits that we had seen hopping about the hillside as we walked on the path above the priory. I did see a few poking their noses out into the June air and nibbling on the grass no doubt sweetened by the recent rain but nowhere near the number I had seen previously. Maybe it wasn't the right time of day. I walked on, making my way through pretty woodland via a path known as The Nun's Causeway to the village of Marrick.

Before I reached Richmond, I passed through another

...y walking
...y husband how he knew
...e had picked up a useful town map
...ad the Coast-to-Coast route marked on it in a
series of boot prints. He also told me that my broken arm had proved useful in knowing that he hadn't missed me. Apparently, he had asked a group of walkers if, 'The lady with the pink pot', was in front of them or behind them. I hadn't realised my arm was becoming famous amongst my fellow walkers.

that I spotted two walkers that I had met up with previously, at various stages of the Coast-to-Coast.

Now so far, I haven't said a lot about my fellow trekkers but as several of us were to congregate in the only pub in Danby Wiske for an evening meal this is a good time to start.

The gentlemen who caught me up in the field, were the ones who had taken my picture on the summit of Dent Fell on the first day. One of the pair was a quiet, pleasant chap who had apparently just retired and had been persuaded by the other one that he needed something to occupy the early days of his leisure so had booked them both onto this holiday. The organiser, and more talkative of the two, who I will call James, was sociable but in a way that, being polite, didn't make you want to spend too long in his company. On that first day he had commented that I seemed to be carrying a lot for just one day and that he had been taught how to carry much less without compromising on efficiency when he had been on some course or other and that as a member of St John's Ambulance Brigade, he could probably reduce the capacity of my first aid kit by at least half. I noticed that he had struggled a little on the ascent of Dent Fell. He brought this up himself, putting it down to having to contracted Lyme Disease some years earlier; I sympathised as the possibility of tick bites is something that I am aware of while walking through damp summer bracken. However, he went on to tell me, he could still remember how to run on the descents as he had been one of the fastest runners on The South Down's Way before he suffered this attack. He went on to prove this by racing ahead down to Nannycatch.

In Borrowdale, on the second day, when I had got into conversation with him again, I was recalling the time when I had canoed in the river there. Of course, this then prompted him to talk about the time he had canoed down the Amazon. I was impressed by his exploits but it did rather take the wind out of my sails and make what I was doing, in undertaking this adventure, seem rather paltry by comparison.

In the beautiful rows of neatly planted vegetables, I was standing in the sunshine admiring the efforts of the farmer, when James crouched down to look more closely at the leaves of the crops and informed me not only that the plants were potatoes but that he knew the exact variety; of course, he was a member of The Market Gardeners Association. Needless to say, I didn't hang around with the pair for long which was a pity as I would have enjoyed walking for a while in the restful company of James's companion. I found an excuse to stop to take photographs of the potato plants and then, in the next field a photo of a beautiful red poppy standing out against the corn, growing tall but still green as it ripened in this well-ordered part of Northern England.

Far from finding this part of the walk tedious, I was finding interest round every corner. After passing under the noisy A1 and an old metal railway bridge I reached Catterick Bridge, a structure apparently unchanged since its construction in 1422. As I used the squeeze stile at the side of the bridge, in contrast to the geometrically planted fields of potatoes, my eyes were greeted by a tangled riot of colourful wild flowers. Tall buttercups and glorious red campion were showing up brightly against the white of the cow parsley and hawthorn hedges. Bolton on Swale was the next village that I reached and it welcomed me in with a table of drinks, biscuits and cakes and an honesty box left for walkers by trusting locals. It made my heart glad that these friendly folks were so tolerant of people wandering through their lovely village. I was making good time so took time to explore the church and the graveyard where I found the imposing monument to Henry Jenkins, a local salmon fisherman whose claim to fame was that he lived to the grand old age of 169. He died in nearby Ellerton in 1670 but apparently remembered being sent, at the age of twelve, with a cartload of arrows to meet the Earl of Surrey's army on its march to The Battle of Flodden in 1513.

After taking photographs and pondering whether I really would want to live as long as Henry, I continued my walk to Danby Wiske. There was more regimented planting in the fields on my route but again my eyes were drawn to the wild flowers at the sides of these fields. There were hedges dotted with dog roses and then as I got nearer to my destination a glorious swathe of bright yellow flag irises. It may have been because Wainwright had led me to expect so little from the walk across The Vale of Mowbray that I looked extra carefully for the positives in the day. Yes, I was looking forward to the Cleveland Hills but I had enjoyed my day.

My hosts for the night were delightful, nothing was too much trouble for them and I felt like I was being treated like family as I sat down for a welcome cup of tea in their garden. After I was changed and ready for my evening meal, I made my way to the pub, less than a hundred yards from their front door. Other Coast-to-Coasters that I recognised were staying at the pub. I was greeted by a lovely couple from Sweden that I had last seen in The Lake District. They were doctors and had commented on my broken arm. I discovered that on the descent to Haweswater from Kidsty Pike, the wife of the couple had taken a tumble and thought for a couple of days that she might have suffered the same injury as me; a broken scaphoid bone. However, after treating it gently and keeping it bandaged, she had decided that, thankfully, her wrist was just badly bruised. They had taken a lot of photographs along the walk but one of their folders of pictures amused me. They had been amazed, early on, by the number of different stiles that they had come across. Consequently, they had made a record of the many ways of crossing walls and fences that they had encountered. I resolved, one day, to look through my own photographs to see how many I could find.

Another couple arrived as we were chatting about stiles. This couple were the ones I probably most admired of all the people I met. Unlike most people undertaking the one hundred- and ninety-two-mile route across Northern England, this couple weren't regular walkers. They had been concerned, at the beginning of the year, that they didn't do enough exercise and had made a New Year's resolution to get fitter. They had started walking their dogs further and going for more local walks. They then decided that they needed a challenge and booked The Coast-to-Coast with a company that would sort out their itinerary, transport their luggage and give them support and advice. They didn't find it easy and the stiles in across The Dales in particular had brought the lady to tears as she struggled to get up and down from them whilst holding the gates open on their, often vicious, hinges. They walked at a steady pace and often got into their digs later than the rest of us but their determination was wonderful and their sense of humour was getting them through. I hope they have gone on to enjoy more challenges together.

James and his companion joined us and true to form, he found something that he had done which gave him one over the rest of us. The pub cat rubbed itself against all our shins in turn and looked up at us longingly until it received a tickle under the chin or behind the ear from each of us. It then proceeded to jump up on James's lap. This apparently wasn't sheer chance; it was because he was the president of his local Cat's Protection League. Oh well! Us mere mortals can only dream of such popularity. I did take a look at his companion and wondered how often during the walk he had turned off his hearing aid and just let John talk to the birds and the trees in the belief that he had an attentive audience.

I had a good night's sleep and was given a tasty breakfast of mushrooms on toast and, because I hadn't eaten as much as my host expected me to eat, was given a lovely packed lunch for free, to send me on my way. I was also delighted by the fact that my host for the coming night was a friend of this lovely couple and they assured me that I would be well looked after in Osmotherly, my next destination.

As I set off, I was amused to see that the first stile I came across was guarded by a couple of rubber rats and above these a carved owl looking down on them from a fence post nearby. I would imagine that a photograph of this fence crossing would make it into the file on the Swedish couple's phone. There was a clear track leading through more pastoral scenery to a railway line which had to be crossed, carefully checking first that no train was in sight. Soon after this obstacle had been negotiated, without a problem, I reached the A19. I had been heartened over the last few miles by the sight of the Cleveland Hills, but if I was to reach them, then this was a hazard that had to be crossed.

I would imagine that if I had walked the twenty- three

miles from Richmond, as Wainwright recommends, (to get this section over with), I would have found it difficult to summon enough energy to cross the tumult of the dual carriage way. It was scary and an unpleasant reminder of the pace of life away from the idyll of this fortnight, when all I had had to think about was continuing to put one foot in front of the other, hopefully in a general Easterly direction. I probably waited longer than necessary for a break in the traffic but I had images running though my head which involved me tripping halfway across and being mown down by a huge lorry and ending more than my walk there and then.

As soon as you leave the thundering traffic, as if to pour balm on your troubled soul, the route takes you through the tranquil village of Ingleby Arncliffe and on to Ingleby Cross. At this point I was in my shorts and t-shirt and was enjoying the June sunshine. I chatted for a few minutes to two lovely ladies who were out walking for the day and had my picture taken at the cross. They walked on while I ate my lunch; looking forward to my first proper ascent for a couple of days.

As I left the village behind, black clouds gathered ominously overhead and my welcome to the North York Moors National Park was a sudden and very heavy downpour. I noticed the ladies that I had met at lunch were obviously not expecting this to be a passing shower and were donning all their waterproof gear, just ahead of me. I decided to do the same. I hadn't got time to visit the nearby Mount Grace Priory but as I started walking uphill following the Cleveland Way, I spotted a small signpost, close to the ground, to the Lady Chapel. I assumed that this would be a ruin associated in some way with that historic site. I decided to investigate. As I ascended the hill following the signpost, taking a detour off route to do so, I was greeted by a series of wooden crosses in amongst the grass and bracken at the side of the path together with plaques carved with, The Stations of The Cross. It was like following a treasure trail and indeed at the top of the hill, I was surprised to find not a ruin but a beautiful old church. I was able to go in out of the rain and spend a few minutes in contemplation before retracing my steps to the onward route to Osmotherly.

I was greeted at the guest house by the friendly lady who knew that I was on my way as she had been speaking to my host from the previous night. I was also pleasantly surprised to see Melissa, with whom I had shared a room in Kirkby Stephen. It was lovely to see her again and share our stories. I love the fact that people doing the Coast-to-Coast vary their itinerary and break their routes at different places but that you are likely to cross paths with the same people several times over the course of your walk.

The Bed and Breakfast in Osmotherly was very homely, to say the least. In fact, I felt as though I was staying in someone's spare room, usually used for family, with all the personal nick-knacks that were around, including hairbrush with someone's curling grey locks spilling out over the dresser. However, the bed was clean and comfortable and our welcome very warm. Our wet clothes and boots were taken away to be dried ready for the next day.

As we walked out for our evening meal, we bumped into the chap from The Netherlands that I hadn't seen since Richmond. He had had a difficult couple of days. The sole had parted company from the upper of one of his walking boots and he had been forced to catch a taxi at one stage. However, he had managed to buy a pair of new boots from the store in Osmotherley and was hoping to be walking again the following day. He had already eaten, so we left him and made our way to the local pub where I was grateful to be able to enjoy my first bowl of pasta with a rich tomato sauce since Borrowdale. While we were eating, Melisssa showed me a picture that she had taken for me; hoping to be able to show me at some stage. It was a photograph of a small lamb, its leg encased in a bright pink plaster just like my own; a sheep to match a Shepherd.

Chapter 21. Climbing again

On leaving our cosy digs the next day, Melissa and I were both presented with a small St Christopher, The Patron Saint of Travellers, to send us on our way. We were very touched by this gesture and felt like we were saying good bye to a kindly aunt, rather than someone we had only known for a few hours.

We walked together for a little while but as Melissa was younger and fitter than I was I suggested that she push on if she wanted to as I didn't want to hold her back. We said our goodbyes, sure that we would meet up again before our challenge was completed.

What a joy it was to be climbing again. The day was perfect; dry, with a gentle breeze and not too hot. I made my way steadily, ascending on clear tracks accompanied by the squeaky toy refrain of lapwings circling the fields alongside the path. This then lead me through a lovely mixed forest where the sweet pine scent of conifers and the shine of holly leaves were interspersed with ancient oaks and horse-chestnuts.

Emerging from the forest at the summit of Beacon Hill I felt my heart lift. This was the type of walking that I was meant for; the effort of climbing being rewarded by views as far as the eye could see. The path was now visible; a neat white scar amongst springy heather, some plants just beginning to show their promise of tiny pink bells. I made a resolution to come and see this sight again in August when this hillside would be dressed in its rose and violet finery. As I write this, I am filled with longing to undertake this wonderful walk again. Maybe one day but for now even going for a walk in the nearby Yorkshire Dales is out of reach as we are currently locked down due to a pandemic which has made armchair walkers of many of us.

I finally reached Carlton Bank; looking between the Boundary Stone and the Ordinance Column at the sharp peak of Roseberry Topping. Any tiredness or weariness that I had felt during the previous one hundred and forty miles or so had disappeared. This felt like the first day again; I was loving this adventure. I made my way down to The Lord Stones Café. This was a rare treat, more so because it is so unexpected to find toilets on route. As I ordered my drink, I spotted Melissa again. I must have made better time than I thought; the adrenalin that had been triggered by a good climb had served me well.

We walked up to Cringle Moor together and enjoyed walking and chatting as we approached The Wainstones. It was great to see these huge rocks and I probably scrambled and played on them more than I needed to.

The name of this book; 'Just Another Pile of Stones' came from the fact that a friend said that most of my pictures were just of piles of stones on top of, 'some mountain or another'. Well, here was a pile of stones that was a bit bigger than most but which felt just as good to reach as the top of Scafell Pike or Ben Nevis.

Before long, it was time to say goodbye again as Melissa took a route off the moor to her accommodation for the night. I walked on to Chop Gate where I was picked up by my lovely host for the night.

I was able to have a bath and change before Peter arrived to take me out for dinner. It was lovely of him to support me in this way as I know he would rather have been walking with me for at least part of the way if he could have done. We had an enjoyable evening which actually resulted in an offer to join the folk group which were practising in the back room of the pub. I had popped my head round a door when I heard them singing; assuming that it was a performance that we were missing. I was invited in and, when the group found that I liked singing, I was given a copy of their music and found myself joining in.

We also chatted to a couple of lads from Belgium who were also doing the Coast to Coast and were staying at the same place as us. This was their second time of doing the trail as they had not finished on the previous occasion. One of the walkers was telling me that he had suffered from severe chafing and walking had become too painful. I sympathised but up to then this was something that hadn't trouble me. After the next day's walking I could have empathised more.

The next day was to be a long walk of about twenty miles but I felt refreshed and ready. I waved Peter off and set off over the North Yorkshire Moors knowing that I only had three more days of my adventure left. There were no route-finding difficulties. The path was clear and the walking easy but I couldn't help wishing that the heather was in bloom as the grey rather parched plants made the scene rather bleak and unattractive. The signs of ancient history that pepper this moorland also made me feel a little uneasy even if they were fascinating. From time to time, I could see other walkers ahead of me which I was grateful for as it wasn't a friendly landscape. The hand stone and the face stone were ancient landmarks that I would normally have been delighted to come across and I am glad I have photos of them but on this particular day, which was grey with a heavy oppressive air, they made me feel unwelcome in a way that I couldn't explain and I had a pang of longing for the friendly fells that I had left behind in the Lake District.

As I took the line of the former Rosedale Ironstone Railway after Bloworth Crossing, the path was coloured a rusty orange in places; a reminder of its iron past. I plodded along this route looking out for sign that I was nearing The Lion Inn where I was hoping to stop for lunch. Perhaps because I didn't have to concentrate on the route and I was not enamoured by the landscape I began to notice that my trousers were rubbing a bit. I remembered our conversation with the Belgium walkers the previous night and tried to put the word 'chafing' out of my mind. My spirits were lifted when, after five miles of following the track-bed of the railway, I spotted the red roof of famous watering hole where lunch was waiting. Even as I approached the building, there was another relic of the past that made me shiver; a depression which had been the site of a cock-fighting pit. I was glad to open the door of the pub and hear the friendly chatter of other walkers and even more delighted to see a familiar face as I looked for a seat. Once again, Melissa and I were able to catch up and share a meal together. A bowl of hot tomato soup hit the spot and I began to feel better than I had all day.

After a good natter and a chance to rearrange my clothing, (hoping that my ongoing walk would be more comfortable than the previous hour had been), Melissa and I set off together. After about fifteen minutes of walking, I suddenly had a sinking feeling; I had left my walking poles at The Lion Inn. As they were new poles, I really didn't want to leave them even though I knew that I could have managed the rest of the walk without them. There was nothing for it but to say my goodbyes to my welcome walking companion and set off back to retrieve my poles from the back of my lunchtime seat in the dark and crowded inn. I wasn't happy to be adding another mile or so to what was already going to be a long day.

I walked out of The Lion alone and for a time I didn't see a soul. I came across Fat Betty, a more friendly landmark than the earlier ones, where offerings of sweets and fruit are left for fellow walkers; and in the spirit of camaraderie with others making this crossing, I left an energy bar and took a wrapped chocolate éclair, enjoying its sweetness as I took pictures of Fat Betty and some crosses erected on the moors by early Christians. Eventually, the views opened up over Great Fryup Dale and I started to feel as though I would make it to Glaisdale. I came across a finger post which told me that the village that I was aiming for was six miles away. While I was pleased to see the sign, my trousers had started chafing again; yes, I had to admit that the discomfort that I was feeling was that which had caused our friends, from the previous night, to curtail their first Coast to Coast journey. Six miles seemed a long way to walk with this frustrating irritation accompanying my every step. To distract myself, I started counting steps but I only usually do that on the last mile of a walk so with six to go it didn't really help. There was nothing for it but to dig in deep, grit my teeth and put one foot in front of the other.

When I eventually reached the village, feeling rather sore and weary, I found a phone box so that I could tell Peter and my Mum that I had made it. Little did I know, even though Wainwright does say Glaisdale is a sprawling village, that my Bed and Breakfast was still a couple of miles away. At the bottom of the main street, I saw some familiar faces outside a pub. It was so lovely to sit down with a glass of refreshing lime and soda clinking with welcome cubes of ice but I didn't stay for long as I was desperate to get to my room for the night and have a shower and a lie down. When I stood up, I began to regret sitting down. I hobbled the rest of the way to my delightful accommodation and was immediately given a cup of tea and piece of cake. A lovely couple that I had last met at Danby Whisk welcomed me, having arrived earlier in the day. They were feeling fresher than me as they had only walked from The Lion Inn that day. They had had their long day earlier in the week.

I was glad to get to my room to take off the offending trousers. After a shower and change of clothes, I felt human enough to join the couple again for a walk to the pub where other faces I recognised were already at their tables. I ate a hearty meal, even managing a dessert which I don't normally indulge in and although I enjoyed listening to the chatter, I was glad when we headed back to our digs and I was able to turn in for an early night.

The next day as I made my way down to breakfast, I was greeted by the hosts of the guest house with the words, 'You look a bit better than you did last night.'

Oh dear! I must have looked as bad as I felt. Luckily, throughout the whole walk, I had found that no matter how tough the previous day had been, I was always eager for the next day's walk. I seemed to recover quickly and unlike many people I don't suffer from blisters which I know can be so debilitating. I had had some problems with painful burning pain under the balls of my feet prior to this trek but the use of insoles had kept this largely at bay.

I probably could have made it from Glaisdale to Robin Hood's Bay but two days of nearly twenty miles didn't seem a good idea when I was doing my planning. I didn't want to finish without any energy left to enjoy the end.

Alfred Wainwright himself agrees;

'... a strong walker could reach Robin Hood's Bay from Glaisdale before nightfall, but country like this is much too good to be hurried over, much too interesting to be appreciated in full measure if limbs are tired...'

My penultimate day therefore, was going to be a short eight miles to Littlebeck, giving me time to linger and think back over my walk.

I made my way out of Glaisdale, stopping to take pictures of the romantic Beggars Bridge, to walk the three and a half miles to Grosmont station. My dad and grandad had both worked for the railway at Horwich Loco Works and Mum had always taken my sister and I to watch the trains after swimming each week so I was glad to have an hour to explore this wonderful piece of history. I walked through the George Stephenson tunnel and wandered into the workshop where the smell of oil and coal brought back childhood memories. I was delighted to watch the engineers working on the steam train, Sir Nigel Gresley, which I hadn't expected.

As I made my way to the end of the platform to continue my walk, another steam train attracted my attention. 'The Lancashire Fusilier' had just come into the station. I felt a real connection with the locomotive and as I saw some passengers alight, I also heard broad

Lancashire accents. I approached these passengers who were obviously part of a large walking group and asked where they were from as the accent was familiar. I smiled as they told me that they were from the Horwich and Chorley walking group; another link with my roots. They had been doing sections of the Coast to Coast for a while as a group and like me were nearing the end of the trail.

I climbed the steep road out of Grosmont, smiling with the thoughts of the unexpectedly happy hour that I just spent, in a place I had previously only read about in my planning guides. I stopped occasionally for a breather, looking back enjoying the retrospective view over The Esk Valley. Luckily the day was clear and as I reached the brow of the hill, Whitby Abbey came into sight as did the East Coast. Wow! The last time I had seen the sea I was turning inland from the wild, wet and windy West Coast near St Bee's lighthouse a fortnight earlier.

A sign soon pointed me in the direction of Littlebeck where I hoped to have a late lunch and a pot of tea, before finding the guest house and going for a wander round this pretty area. However, this wasn't to be. Littlebeck is a very pretty hamlet but there was no sign of a café, pub or even a small shop where I could buy lunch. I should have checked but I always carry spare food in case of emergencies so I found a handy bench with a scenic view and unpacked my apple, crisps and some nuts and raisins. Luckily after such a short day of walking this meagre fare was more than sufficient to replenish the calories spent and water would have to do to quench my thirst. Still feeling full of walking, I decided to walk a section of the final day's route. This took me into a beautiful wood which was a magical place. Looking at Wainwright's Coast to Coast he has this to say about Littlebeck:-

'*Littlebeck, a miniature Arcadia embowered in trees, a*

glimpse of heaven for nerve-frayed town- dwellers.'

It was so peaceful, walking by the water amongst the trees knowing that I only had one day left to walk to Robin Hood's Bay, that I was able to reflect on the last one hundred and eighty miles. I remember at one point, sitting on a large boulder watching the water gently lapping near my boots while birds sang in the branches all around me and becoming quite teary. At that moment, I didn't want the trail to end. I think, if someone had said at that point that they had booked the accommodation and if I fancied turning round at the end and heading back to St Bees then I could, that I would have jumped at the chance. It was in this melancholy mood that I made my way to the lovely Intake Farm.

I was greeted with a pot of tea and a delicious piece of home-made Bakewell Tart.

As there was nowhere to eat in Littlebeck, Judith, the host offered her guests a lovely home-cooked meal at a large sociable table. Everyone was chattering about their experiences and reflecting on the fact they were nearly at the end. After our meal, Judith told us that there was a charity concert in the hamlet that evening. I decided that I would enjoy something a bit different and another guest, the Dutch walker that I had met a couple of times previously, also chose to accept the invitation. We talked on the way to the concert and I discovered that he enjoyed walking in the UK as he liked hills which of course are in short supply in The Netherlands. The outdoor concert made for a delightful evening which was rounded off perfectly for me with songs from my favourite musical, Les Miserables.

However, this was one of those evenings when you wish you could have been in two places at once. When we returned to the farm the other guests were just gathering up a number of OS Maps. They had spent their evening putting out all the OS maps which contained sections of the route of the Coast to Coast and following the journey that they had taken to reach this point. I had used the Harvey's Maps which are linear and easier to carry but it would have been great to see the route spread out in its entirety.

I wasn't sure how I felt when I woke the next morning. I was looking forward to seeing my husband and to sleeping in my own bed that night but I wasn't enjoying the fact that I would be returning to the busyness of normal life. I would be back at work the following day. I was teaching a lovely class at the time but the routine of a school day had much less appeal than a day walking through beautiful forests beside star filled streams, accompanied by birdsong.

Chapter 22.
The end

I was able to relax into my day's walking as I had already checked out the route the previous day. I had no need to hurry and I could stop to enjoy the points of interest in the woods before I left the path through the trees. The Hermitage is a fascinating shelter carved from one huge piece of rock. I sat inside for a while, understanding totally why someone might want to escape the rat race and live simply in a little stone home; though there is no evidence that anyone actually ever lived there.

Soon after leaving this little hobbit home, I could hear

the unmistakeable sound of water falling from a height and sure enough, though the trees I could see the milky whiteness of Falling Foss. Emerging from the forest, I made my way to Hawkser. I found a pub where I had a bowl of soup among family groups out for their Sunday Lunch. I felt out of place sitting in my dusty walking shorts and muddy boots when other diners were dressed in their Sunday clothes so I didn't stay long. Before long I was walking along the cliff path. I stopped to take a photo of the sea and was caught by my Dutch friend again. He expressed his surprise and confusion that the sea was on his left as it had been on the very first day. He felt happier when I explained that for the first few miles we had walked West before turning inland. All of a sudden, we spotted Robin Hood's Bay; the end was in sight. As solo walkers we agreed that we would finish the walk alone so I let him walk ahead of me while I took more photographs of the scene.

I soon reached the steep street descending to Robin Hood's Bay. This scene had been etched on my memory since childhood though I had rarely visited. A cine film taken by a family friend when I was about four or five had recorded for posterity the moment that I had dropped my bright red plastic bucket and it had rolled away down the cobbles. The joy of this film though was that it was often played backwards to make me laugh as my bucket seemingly defied gravity and rolled up the hill and jumped into my hand.

I was thinking about this when I suddenly spied my daughters walking up the street on the opposite side of the road. I was delighted that they had obviously joined Peter to welcome me for the finale of my walk. They glanced my way but continued walking without acknowledging

Coast to coast with a pink pot

me until I shouted and waved. After giving me wonderful congratulatory hugs, they told me that they had spotted me and Hannah had said, 'That lady looks like Mum but I guess she's just setting off; she doesn't look tired enough to have walked one hundred and ninety miles.' They were amazed to find that I wasn't hobbling and actually still looked well and happy.

Peter was waiting at the car and had champagne and a balloon with congratulations emblazoned across it. After kisses and more hugs, he told me that there was a further surprise waiting for me. About a dozen friends from our church had driven to Robin Hood's Bay to help me celebrate. They had gone for a short walk; not expecting me to arrive so early.

I walked down the slipway and having dug the little pebble that I had chosen in St Bees from the depths of my rucksack I launched it into the North Sea. As I walked back towards the main street, I recognised the group friends who had gathered to offer their congratulations. As we chatted and shared the bubbly, clouds gathered and it started to rain. We headed to a nearby coffee shop and ordered tea and cake while I relaxed in the knowledge that I had completed the trail.

Eventually, Peter, the girls and I were left alone to make our way back to the car.

I had a mix of feelings, joy at being back with my family, a certain relief touched with pride at having got to the end of The Coast to Coast safely and a sadness that my adventure was over.

I am sure many adventurers understand the slightly flat and deflated feeling that accompanies the elation of success. Life had to get back to normal but I was now a

Coast to Coaster like thousands of others before me. I did realise on my way home that I hadn't signed the book in the pub at the end of the trail; oh well maybe I'll just have to do it all again one day.

Chapter 23.
Sore feet, bunions and hammer toes

You may be forgiven for thinking that I must be one of those lucky people who never suffer with the painful foot conditions that hamper many walkers; this couldn't be further from the truth.

During the last few Wainwrights. I had had problems with a burning pain that would attack the balls of my feet from time to time. It would vary in severity from a discomfort that felt like my socks were bunched up behind my toes to feeling like I was trying to walk with a burning iron bar inside my boots. The pain could last anything from a couple of minutes to a couple of hours. Feeling frustrated by this pain, I sought the advice of a local chiropodist who made me some insoles which I could wear inside my shoes and boots. These were a huge help and though they didn't stop the problem entirely, they made it manageable and certainly helped me to cope with the distances needed to complete the Coast to Coast without too many incidences of the severe burning pain. However, my foot problems were far from over.

The days following my epic walk saw my feet swelling up like puddings. This was something new. When I was struggling to fasten my shoes, I decided that I ought to visit the GP. I was given tablets to bring the swelling down and anti-histamines which she felt would also help. Over the next fortnight, my feet shrunk back to their normal size but I was told that, should I ever want to do a long distance walk again, that next time I should wear compression socks!

I also noted, around the same time that my hammer toes (inherited from my dad) were becoming more pronounced and therefore more likely to rub, so whilst seeing me about the swollen feet, my GP decided to refer me to a specialist about both the pains I had been having and the hammer toes.

When I eventually got to see the foot specialist, he did ultra sound scans on my feet and diagnosed me with Moreton's Neuromas. He also looked at the hammer toe and developing bunion on my left foot and decided that he could deal with all three conditions if I was to consent to surgery. Desperate for pain free feet, I readily agreed. I did manage to do quite a bit of walking in the year between the end of the Coast to Coast and the foot surgery the following year, using my insoles and taping up my toes so they wouldn't rub.

Once I knew that I was going under the knife, I did start panicking that I might never be able to do any serious walking again. I kept seeing accounts of walks in The Lake District that I hadn't done and wanted to do. One of these was a route up Pavey Ark in The Langdales called Jack's Rake. I read Wainwright's comments in his Central Fells Pictorial Guide.

'As a walk, it, (Jack's Rake), is both difficult and awkward: in fact, for much of the way the body is propelled forwards by a series of convulsions unrelated to

normal walking, the knees and elbows contributing as much to progress as hands and feet. Walkers who can put their toes in their mouths and bring their knees up to their chins may embark upon this ascent confidently; others unable to perform these tests, will find the route difficult.'

I diligently tried the tests that Wainwright advised: yes, my toes did reach my mouth and my knees could with some assistance from my arms be pulled up to my chest. However, I also researched other routes just in case I changed my mind.

I drove up to The New Dungeon Ghyll in Great Langdale on a day that promised sunshine and good views after rain on the previous day. I chatted in the car-park to a National Trust Warden who was there trying to enlist support for the organisation. I told him of my plans and he said that I shouldn't attempt the rake as it would be very wet from the previous day's downpour. He did say, 'It will still be there another day, when conditions are better.' This didn't particularly encourage me as, at that stage, I didn't know whether there would be another day post-op for me to tackle it.

I walked up the steep but steady route from the hotel to the beautiful, Sprinkling Tarn which always makes one breathe more easily and has the magical ability to eliminate stress and worry. I was standing by the low wall pondering the route up Jack's Rake across the gently rippling water.

I was aware of several people having a discussion and pointing out the various routes. One of the men turned to me and said, 'Are you doing it then?'. I told him that I had been advised not to and he admitted that some members of their group were heeding that warning and giving Jack's Rake a miss. However, four of them were going to go for it. They asked if I wanted to join them. I did say that I was tempted and they assured me that they would help me if I needed it and that they weren't at all worried that I might slow them down. These weren't young whipper-snappers but gentlemen of a similar age to me who just fancied getting this climb under their belts. I made the decision to join them.

Unfortunately, I don't have many pictures of the climb as I packed my camera, route map and walking poles into my rucksack so as to leave my hands completely free for negotiating the various rocky handholds that I would need to use on the ascent. Initially, I absolutely loved the climb and because you are climbing inside a sort of chimney didn't feel any sense of exposure as we climbed high above Sprinkling Tarn. We reached the rowan tree, famous for being a good mid-climb resting point, and although I had needed all my concentration to reach this spot, I was enjoying the climb. I had a huge grin on my face as I climbed onto the grassy platform where we could take a breather and enjoy the breath-taking views. One member of the group did capture this grin with his camera and I do look remarkably relaxed in the photograph.

My legs were stretching and bending, as Wainwright had suggested they would need to, quite happily but then one large step loomed up in front of me and seemed impossible to surmount. I couldn't find a handhold that would give me enough grip to ensure I was secure as I hauled myself up to the next safe place for my right foot. After several attempt to lift my right leg further than it wanted to go, I had to admit defeat; I needed some help here. One of the men in the group was directly above me and managed to secure himself so that he could reach down and secure my hand, with his, on a strong outcrop of rock. With my hand firmly secured; I then called from a push from below, just to propel my leg further than it would spring without assistance. This worked and I was on my way once more. I was so glad that I hadn't attempted this climb on my own. I might have become one of the many 'crag fast' climbers who have to be rescued by the selfless men and women of the Mountain Rescue service.

I said a fond farewell to the four men, who had helped me to achieve a grade one scramble, as they went off to join the rest of their party, and went on with my walk. I must have been feeling a bit wobbly from my experience as I walked directly to Harrison Stickle, missing out the summit of Thunacar Knott which had been on my itinerary, and onto the lovely Pike O' Stickle. This wonderful fell, with its distinctive rounded pyramidal shape which can be seen for miles around, has an exciting little scramble of its own but has the last laugh when you see that the descent is an easy series of rock steps and that getting hands on to haul yourself to the summit was completely unnecessary, but fun. Loft Crag was my last fell of the day and I made my way back to the New Dungeon Gill only to find my good Samaritans enjoying a well-deserved pint. I was invited to join them for a de-brief of the day and to share contact details so that we could share the photos of the day as reminders of a wonderful day. This was a route that I am unlikely to repeat but I was so glad that I had decided to do it that day.

It was interesting to note that the stomach-churning fear of heights and tingling feet only kicked in when I was watching other people's videos of their experiences on The Rake which I found on the following evening when I was trying to show Peter what I had done. My body and mind had served me well, keeping these things at bay long enough for me to enjoy a real rock climb albeit a fairly simple one as far as real rock climbers are concerned.

Chapter 24.
The Six Dales Trail

I also walked The Six Dales Trail with Hannah, my eldest daughter, just before my scheduled surgery.

The Six Dales Trail is a thirty-eight mile walk from Otley in Wharfdale to Middleham in Wensleydale. The other dales it visits are Wasburndale, Nidderdale, Colsterdale and Coverdale. Hannah had her own personal reasons for choosing the weekend that she wanted to do her first ever long distanced walk and, in spite of my feet, she was sure I'd be fine! Peter dropped us in Otley to start the walk and was due to pick us up at the end of the day at Fewston reservoir about ten miles away. After leaving the streets on the outskirts of Otley we had a lovely walk over fields and along ancient tracks except for one heat-stopping moment when a herd of cows took a distinct dislike to us and another couple of walkers also on the trail. They were a mixed herd with calves and a bull amongst them; the most dangerous mix. Walking very quickly away from them and in the wrong direction for our onward path, we managed to climb over a metal farm gate and get ourselves to safety. After consulting the map, we decided to walk round the field on the road in order to get back onto our route. Apart from this little drama we had a lovely day and when we got to Fewston, we realised that we still had some miles in our legs and walked another couple of miles to Thruscross reservoir where our 'taxi' was waiting.

We were returning back to base each evening so that Hannah could get home to see to her cats and sleep in her own bed.

We were so glad that we had chosen to add the couple of miles to our first day's walking as we woke on the second day to torrential rain. We were in full waterproofs as we set off for Patley Bridge. There were some joyful scenes that kept us smiling in spite of the rain. There was a beautiful and unexpected tarn in the middle of a wood; Guisecliff Tarn; a field, full of Wensleydale sheep with their wonderfully long curly locks, also being enjoyed by a huge flock of grey lag geese and the lovely riverside path into Pateley Bridge. On reaching this village we took the opportunity to have our lunch in a dry café rather than eat our sandwiches in the rain. They would do for the following day. We walked our last leg of the day by Gowthwaite Reservoir to be picked up in Ramsgill ready to be taken home to dry out and recover for day three.

Day three dawned much brighter and Hannah and I were soon climbing onto Low Ash Head Moor and some wonderful long ranging views. This was a great open expanse of moor and both of us enjoyed this section of the walk. Hannah was getting a bit tired by this time but was still doing well for someone who doesn't enjoy hills. There was an unexpected highlight to come though. After passing though the pretty village of Ellerstring, we walked on a beautiful sunken pathway towards Jervaulx Abbey. As we crossed a stile at the end of the pathway, we emerged onto a road immediately opposite one of Hannah's favourite places; Brymore Ice Cream Parlour and tea shop.

We had a welcome pot of tea and each chose our ice creams from the extensive menu before setting out to walk through the ruins of the abbey. Our route then led us onto an attractive riverside path by banks of the River Cover. We were nearly at the end of our walk. There was one final instruction that made Hannah's face drop; 'ascend across fields towards Middleham'. The lack of a signpost at the bottom of this field made her doubt that the field I was turning into was the right one. Hannah didn't want to put one foot uphill if she didn't have to so she sent me ahead to check. Luckily after fifty yards or so, I spotted a way-marker on the wall and was able to reassure her that I was on the right path. I waited for her to catch me up and we made our way to the brow of the hill to be greeted by the majestic site of Middleham Castle. We walked down beside the castle walls to the market cross where our walk reached its conclusion.

I was amazed that my feet had held out and that I had completed another long walk. Hannah was exhausted but very proud of herself even though she didn't even feel able to walk around the village in search of a tea shop. Hannah is a vegetarian and careful not to consume meat products usually asking for chips cooked in sunflower oil. However, it was a measure of her hunger and exhaustion that when I offered to buy her some chips from the chip shop near The Market Cross where were sitting, she said in desperation, 'Oh! Yes, please and I don't even mind if they are made of cow!'

After this walk, my thoughts began to turn to my upcoming surgery and I reflected that, even if I couldn't walk for a while, I had plenty of photographs and memories to be looking through until I was able to plan my next adventure.

Chapter 25.
Surgery and recovery

My surgery went ahead as planned and as instructed I used crutches and a large boot to get around for the next few weeks, looking forward to the day when my new correctly shaped and pain-free foot would be revealed.

I was actually feeling quite hopeful and excited as I went to have the bandage and pins removed. My husband accompanied me to the appointment and we arranged to go out for lunch afterwards. However, the actual reality of the appointment was very different. The removal of the pins and stitches was more painful than I had expected and the surgeon told me that he hadn't been able to remove the neuromas. He did say that he thought the bunion and hammer-toe work had gone well though so all was not lost. We went home instead of out for the planned celebratory lunch and I spent the rest of the day feeling rather crestfallen.

My recovery was slow and when I was finally able to get my foot into my walking boot, I made my way around a familiar path on a local hill; Otley Chevin. I walked not like a peak bagger but like someone on their last legs.

I am by nature an up-beat, positive person so I started to plan some gentle walks.

I had to get back to my beloved Lakes and get my mojo back so I started to look at Wainwright's book 'The Outlying Fells of Lakeland'.

The front cover of this volume declares it to be: -

'A Pictorial Guide to the lesser fells around the perimeter of Lakeland written primarily for old age

pensioners and others who can no longer climb the high fells but who can still, within reason, potter about on the short and easy slopes and summits of the foothills.'

As pottering seemed to be all I was capable of, this seemed a good way to get my hill fix without pushing my foot too far. In the middle of September 2012, just over two months after my operation, Peter drove me up to the South Eastern Marches of the Lake District to climb at least one and hopefully two of the fells in the book that I had been studying; Hugill Fell and Reston Scar from the village of Staveley. Both of these fells are a mile from bottom to top and use the same line for ascent and descent. This would mean that I wouldn't risk extending the walk beyond my capabilities and that I could give up after the first one if there was a problem.

The first fell I climbed was Hugill Fell. As the track passed a bungalow, I was greeted by a friendly and very lively black and white spaniel. It's owner, who was gardening, introduced the dog as Jess. He asked if I was just going up and down the fell and when I said I was, he asked if I wanted company. It turned out that Jess loved to accompany walkers up her local fell. I was a bit worried that I was now responsible for this bundle of energy. I needn't have worried, she was brilliant. She kept running ahead and rounding back and checking on me every few minutes. There was an amusing moment when we reached what was obviously the summit of this little hill but there was no sign of the shapely cairn sketched by Wainwright in his inimitable style. Jess was sitting looking up at me with a satisfied look that turned to confusion when I said, 'Find the top, Jess. Where's the cairn?'. After exploring the surrounding hillside, I decided that the cairn was nowhere to be found and with one word, 'Home',

Jess led me back to the bungalow and my waiting husband. Jess was returned to her owner a lot muddier than she had left but well exercised. When I asked about the cairn, I was told that it had been dismantled to make a path over the bog after some recent heavy rain. I am sure it was rebuilt as the ground dried out but Jess was my marker for the summit of my first post-op fell.

I had enjoyed my little jaunt and decided that I could manage Reston Scar as well. The hills of The Lake District were working their magic on my mood and my feet. My foot felt better than it had in months. I was back!

Even though my feet seemed to enjoy being in my hiking boots, I was still in agony in my everyday shoes. Walking round the shops, never my favourite hobby any time, had me in tears. I went back to work but, still in pain, I was referred back to the consultant who had done my operation who in turn referred me to his orthotist who looked at all my various shoes and boots and at the insoles I had used on the Coast to Coast and decided he could help me. After taking various measurements he made me some new insoles. They did improve things a little but I still wasn't right. Throughout the winter I returned to the orthotist several times until finally being discharged. I just did local walks when I could, but it was February the following year before I felt ready to tackle any walks on my own again. I was comforted by the fact that my hiking boots were the only things my feet were anything near comfortable in.

I decided that even though I didn't think I could manage anything like the walks I had been doing prior to my operation, I still needed a challenge so I thought I would complete Wainwright's Outlying Fells of Lakeland, as I had already made a start with Hugill Fell and Reston

Scar.

For one small volume there are a surprising number of summits; one hundred and sixteen in all. I thought these would keep me out of mischief for a while.

I returned to Staveley and climbed High Knott on the first bright day of February 2013. I contoured the little fell until I found a tiny squeeze stile to gain access to the summit. This was so small that I had to leave my rucksack behind. I have since learned that this gap in the wall has now been blocked off and access to the summit of this fell is now impossible; I was lucky. I then went on to climb School Knott and Grandsire from Ings. I had had a good day and my feet had held out.

I had a new target and I suppose I should have been satisfied with that but I was still

desperate to do what I thought of as a decent walk. I was looking at Wainwright's 'Walks in Limestone Country' which I had been given by the kind friends who had accompanied me on my final Wainwright.

On the front of the book were three interesting looking cairns; The Three Men of Gragareth. I decided that I fancied visiting this 'noble landmark', as Wainwright describes it and as soon as the forecast looked promising, I downloaded a walk which visited these cairns and the summits of three fells over two thousand feet and set off. The day was very cold but still and bright; my favourite walking weather. Unfortunately, I followed my Sat-Nav to the start of this walk and the route it took was winding and long and resulted me being held up by some road works but once there I donned my boots and set off. I climbed to three cairns which looked wonderful against the clear blue winter sky. My onward route followed a wall over frozen ground. I have since met people who have declared this walk, boggy and featureless. I was lucky, the bogs and snow layer were frozen solid so I could simply walk over the top of them. I climbed Gragareth, Green Hill and Great Coum, descended to and crossed Ease Gill before it disappeared underground at a sink hole leaving me to walk back to my car along a dry river bed. Maybe it was the freezing ground or just the fact that I was concentrating on my route but I had managed the walk without too much pain at all.

Perhaps what I needed was another challenge to do alongside, 'The Outlying Fells of Lakeland'.

Chapter 26.
The Nuttalls

Since I had completed the Wainwrights, something that a friend had said in passing had niggled at me. She had commented that not all the high mountains of England were in The Lake District. There were some big fells in the North Pennines which could compete in stature with some of the biggest Lakeland fells and why didn't I do those? I must admit, I hadn't really looked beyond Lakeland and my local area for walks and felt somewhat naïve as I realised that Cross Fell was only just below Great Gable in height and was in fact the thirteenth highest mountain in England. I started to look at other two thousand footers. There were a lot of them and many outside Lakeland. I discovered that these fells had been climbed and logged by a couple named John and Anne Nuttall who had classified a group of fells under their name;

Nuttalls are defined as peaks above 2,000 feet

(609.6m) in height, the general requirement to be called a 'mountain' in the British Isles, and with a prominence above 15 metres (49.2 ft)

I had obviously made a good start on this list with the Wainwrights and was pleased that I had added tops to my Wainwright walks, such as Symonds Knott near Scafell and Black Sails near Wetherlam, both of which qualified for a place in this new list of peaks. This was what I needed to get the adrenaline pumping again and gave me a reason to fight my foot problems rather than give in to them. My Gragareth walk had given me three fells to add to the list and I started looking for more.

I was working more or less full time again by this stage as Peter and I were supporting the girls at university, so walks were restricted to weekends and holidays but I was determined to get back to my peak bagging exploits whenever I could.

Sore feet? What sore feet? I wish I had been able to forget about them but I became a bit of a puzzle to my friends. I would need to use the car just to go to the local shops and would have to cut short shopping trips because I couldn't walk another step and yet would lace up my boots and complete a twelve- mile hike. I found this confusing too but put it down to my feet being held better in my boots than in any other footwear. I wasn't complaining; I was just glad it was that way round. The Peak Bagger was back.

My next Nuttall proved a bit tricky. I had done Penyghent a few times but hadn't ever gone over to Plover Hill. This walk wouldn't involve too much driving and the route finding would be fine as I had done most of the walk before. As with the Gragareth walk, the ground was frozen which made for good progress across what would usually be boggy ground from the smallest of the three Yorkshire peaks to the new summit. Although the summit cairn was over a wall which had to be climbed via a stile type contraption at a junction of two walls, I had no trouble reaching it but my onward path proved a little more difficult. There are steep rock steps down off Plover Hill reached by a grassy descent. As soon as I started to descend, I realised I had a problem. I needed crampons if I wasn't to go flying over the edge of the rock face into which the promised steps had been cut. As I hadn't brought the necessary footwear, I was about to give up and turn round to head back for Penyghent and the clear Pennine Way path back to Horton in Ribblesdale when I heard the voices of some other walkers.

The leader of the group was a confident chap who knew where the steps were and didn't think that there would be a problem reaching them. I did try to say that I had tried but he was determined to follow his planned route. However, after trying various ways, he had to admit that the chosen line of descent was impassable. At one point I sat down on the ice to prevent myself from slipping. When I came to stand up, I really struggled. I really didn't fancy flying over the rocks and was a bit nervous as I just couldn't get and purchase with my boots. I needed to stay with the group though to be safe so made a real effort to dig my poles into the ice and push myself to my feet. We walked across the face of the fell, parallel to the edge of the rocks until we reached some softer snow in a less rocky area. We made a plan to kick steps in the snow to get us to the lower path. With us all helping, we made short work of making a diagonal set of steps down to a lower path which was clear of ice and only had a light sprinkling of snow. After this we were able to make good time back to Horton in Ribblesdale and the end of the walk.

Over Easter, Peter and I popped over to the Lakes so that I could bag another couple of Outlying Fells. Whitbarrow was one that I really enjoyed, as there aren't many places in The Lake District where you find limestone pavements. I loved the array of hawthorn trees bent by the wind and juniper bushes set against the outcrops of dazzling white limestone.

Wainwright has high praise for this little fell and says that;

'The walk described is the most beautiful in this book; beautiful it is every step of the way. It includes a traverse of the finest scar top and returns through delightful woods along the base of the cliffs. After initial steepness the walking is exceedingly pleasant, in surroundings high above encircling valleys and amidst scenery that has no blemish. All is fair to the eye on Whitbarrow.'

Having completed all the outlying fell walks in Wainwright's book, I have other walks which to my mind would compete for the title of the most beautiful but at this stage I had to agree with the great man; this was a wonderful walk. Peter came to collect me from Beck Head where we found a welcome surprise. There was a refreshment barn with a large urn of hot water to make coffee and tea and a selection of cakes to choose from. There was an honesty box for payment and we relaxed to enjoy this treat together in the welcome spring sunshine.

The next little fell took longer to find than it did to walk. We imagined Cartmel Fell would be climbed from the small town of Cartmel, famous for its sticky toffee pudding. After parking up by the church and looking round for the fell to no avail, we looked more carefully at the map. We realised that the tiny Cartmel Fell Church, that lies at the foot of this fell, was some way from the town. We set off and were soon parked up by the right church. Peter didn't even have time to finish a sudoku puzzle while I climbed to the well- built cairn, admired the lovely views over The Winster Valley to larger snow-capped fells beyond, came down again and explored the ancient church. I was glad I hadn't made a special trip to The Lakes just to bag this one but with Whitbarrow the day before it had been a lovely little trip.

I had bagged a few fells since my operation but didn't really feel as though I had tested myself properly so I looked for walks that would bag me some more of the desired mountains in the Nuttalls' list but were easy enough to get to. On my drives up to The Lake District I had seen the rolling fells of The Howgills on the left of the M6, as I drove towards the A66 for Keswick, but had never ventured onto their lonely looking slopes.

As I researched my next walk, I discovered one that would take me up by England's highest waterfall, Cautley Spout. This looked quite spectacular on pictures that I found and although the ascent looked steep, I thought that the waterfall would be a good distraction from sore feet and aching limbs.

I parked near The Cross Keys just outside Sedbergh. This is a fascinating establishment which would be a disappointment to many walkers, looking for a welcome pint as a reward for a day's walking, as it is a temperance inn, serving no alcohol at all. However, a look at its drinks' menu would take many people back to their childhood in the 1960's when wonderful names such as dandelion and burdock, cream soda and sarsaparilla had our mouths watering and pocket money burning a hole in our pockets. The Cross Keys also allowed walkers to use their loo for a small donation; something which I wish other establishments would do. Too often I have felt obliged to buy an unwanted drink at the start of a walk just so that I could answer the call of nature before I set off.

The climb up the waterfall was steep but exhilarating, even though I did have to stand still and steady myself occasionally as it was a dizzying experience. When I reached the top of the falls, I was fascinated to see an Andy Goldsworthy sheep pen at the side of my onward path. I had been teaching one of my classes about his art but never expected to come across a piece in these remote hills.

I had chosen this route because it was a short walk that bagged me five Nuttalls. What I should have realised from the fact that the time suggested for this walk was five hours was that the six miles were likely to be thigh and feet burning ones. I coped well until The Calf and was entertained at this particular summit by a cyclist who decided to pose for a photograph on the trig point. It is not unusual for people to climb onto these structures but this particular gentleman went one step further and held his bicycle above his head for the summit shot. Rather him than me; it was a very windy day and hard enough to stand still to take a picture.

My route then dropped down into Bowderdale Beck before climbing up Yarlside. Suddenly, I started to feel the unwelcome twinge in my feet and as I started the pathless climb, the fire started. It took me much longer than it should have done to climb this final fell of the day. I pushed on but didn't enjoy this summit at all. My descent was done largely on my backside as every time I put either foot down it felt like I was being stabbed in the balls of my feet by sharp knives. I made my way back to the Cross Keys, hobbling as I had done after a twenty -mile day on the Coast to Coast. I took a trip down memory lane with a drink of cream soda at the inn before taking my boots off and releasing my poor feet. They throbbed and cramped before they settled enough for me to put my trainers on and start the drive back to Leeds.

I worried that I had done some harm to my feet but after a bath and a good night's sleep I was glad to find that I had done no lasting damage.

Chapter 27.
To walk or not to walk? That was the question

You will have your own ideas about what I should have done at this stage

There will be those who are looking for encouragement to keep walking in spite of age, lack of confidence or aches and pains like mine. On the other hand, there will be people who think that, with the pain I was having, I should probably have called it a day. Those who walk in the mountains will understand that the draw of the fells is so strong that it pushes you to climb them whether or not you should.

In spite of the agony that I had felt on Yarlside, looking back at my photos made me realise what I would have missed if I had not walked that day; the magnificent Cautley Spout; the Andy Goldsworthy sculpture; the dare devil cyclist on the trig point of The Calf and that wonderful taste of cream soda.

I was going to carry on. I had set myself some new challenges and I was determined not to be beaten.

I decided to try another long walk but without the steep ups and downs of The Howgills. I thought it might be good to do some walks in the Yorkshire Dales. I chose a thirteen-mile walk which, unlike Yarlside, had clear paths; partly on The Herriot Way and partly on The Pennine Way. The walk took me to the summits of Great Shunner Fell and Lovely Seat. The start of the walk though fields of knee-high buttercups reminded me of the beautiful countryside through Reeth and Richmond on the Coast to Coast. The walk was long but it wasn't difficult and the pain in my feet came and went throughout the day but was never unbearable.

I followed this walk the next month with another glorious Dales' route to Fountains Fell and Darnbrook Fell. The scenery, wild flowers, wild strawberries, cotton grass and the lively fell ponies that I saw that day, made me even more determined to fight on.

Peter was happy to encourage my exploits knowing that fell-bagging made me happy and he would have a more contented wife than if I was sitting at home nursing my painful feet and fretting.

We started planning our summer holiday and decided to go and visit The North Pennines so that I could climb Cross Fell and some other Nuttalls that were in the top forty highest in England. I had been warned that it was rare to have clear views from the top of Cross Fell and that I would be lucky not to be walking in mist and murk when I tried to bag them. I also heard tales of the Helm Wind that often makes walking difficult and causes these particularly bad conditions. This didn't stop us booking a cottage near Alston in the hope that I could get some Nuttalls under my belt.

The weather forecast for the week wasn't good but we were extremely lucky, it rained every night but each day dawned quite bright and stayed fine for most of the days that we were there. The area was beautiful. Walking out from the cottage in Nenthead, I could walk by a river edged with harebells and long waving grasses to a surprising cottage garden filled with carefully crafted miniature buildings many of which I recognised from The Lake District. Someone had patiently reconstructed the tiny Bridge House in Ambleside and other landmarks, making a wonderful display that I went to visit a couple of times during the week. Without my urge to walk anywhere and everywhere I wouldn't come across these little gems but this was a delightful find. I also had an afternoon walk from the little village of Garrigill to the picturesque Ashgill Falls. This is an amazing waterfall and one that you can walk behind to get a magical view through the curtain of tumbling water.

I chose the best day of week for the ascent of Cross Fell. It was a bright windy day and I felt ready for the climb ahead. For once I couldn't just follow a walk route from my favourite website; their walk to bag the three fells that I had in my sight was a twenty miler and I didn't feel that my feet were ready for that; especially in an unfamiliar area. I decided that after all the time I had spent looking at maps, I should be able to work out my own route. I did start from Kirkland following a go4awalk route and was surprised and quite excited to see a Wainwright's Pennine Journey signpost; that made me feel at home. Although the wind was strong, it was exhilarating rather than a problem. I was so lucky, when I reached the summit of Cross Fell, I could see for miles and miles across to my beloved Lakeland. What a privilege; one that so many walkers have been denied. I could clearly see my onward route to Great and Little Dunn Fells. As I walked, the cotton grass, blowing in the strong wind, looked so beautiful that I sat down among the white waving strands to look at the most wonderful panorama. The picture that I took is a pale reminder of that glorious view.

After visiting the summit of Great Dunn Fell adorned with its huge white radar domes, oddly out of place amidst the cotton grass, and the wonderfully named Dun Fell Hush, I had to make my way down to a little village called Millburn. I had asked Peter to pick me up from there. Although the path wasn't as clear as it had appeared on the map, I was able match a small plantation that I could see in the distance with one on the map and follow some walls to make my way safely down to my waiting taxi and my very patient husband. I was quite pleased to have used my own map-reading skills and a route of my own devising to bag three of the highest Nuttalls outside The Lake District.

Two days later I set out to climb Murton Fell, another Nuttall, from Dufton, where Peter found a pub, where he could spend some time, that had WiFi, served food and sold a good pint and which was aptly named, The Shepherd's Inn. I was attracted to the walk to bag Murton Fell by the walk description which said it would take me to England's Grand Canyon which would be 'Truly Spectacular'.

I set off on the right route but somewhere alongside a small stream called Trundale Gill I lost my way. I was quickly learning that paths on the North Pennine maps, unlike those leading to Wainwright summits, are not clear stony tracks trodden by hundreds of feet but are often grassy sheep trods that fizzle out from time to time. I set my compass and trudged up a grassy bank out of an increasingly deep ravine to reach its head. I thought it would be easy once I was back on track. All I had to do was to, 'Walk South East across the grass to the summit of Murton Fell'. Grass- this was a very sanitised word for the terrain that I had to cross. I ended up jumping from one small peaty mound to another and crossing tussocks of rough grass while trying to follow my compass bearing. This was not easy. The fell top is flat so the summit not at all distinct. It was by sheer luck that I spotted a small mound of stones perched on yet another small mound of peat. I let out a cry of, 'Thank goodness for that' and set off on my merry way. It wasn't long before I spotted a tall stone beacon and made a bee line for that and for the stone throne a few metres away. Within half an hour I was on the Pennine Way and I spotted my first walkers of the day, sensibly keeping to the main, well-trodden, highway.

I knew I was looking forward to seeing High Cup Nick but nothing could have prepared me for the breath-taking sight. I know many people travel far and wide to see wonders of the natural world and of course many are deeper, higher, older and in many ways more spectacular than anything we have here in Britain. However, this wonderful deep chasm on a lonely Pennine fellside doesn't announce itself with tourist shops, cafes and high-cost entry fees. It is reserved for those prepared to don their boots and walk up the rough track above the small, but perfectly formed, village of Dufton. The route that I took meant that this wonderful sight was hidden until the very last minute when I could stand at the head of the huge gorge and wonder at the almost a geometrically perfect U-shaped chasm formed by glaciers in successive ice ages. All the trudging up grass and jumping over peat were forgotten as I stood feeling very small, awestruck by what I was seeing. My camera snapped away as I tried, in vain to capture the sight. Eventually, I tore myself away and walked back, along a path above High Cup Nick, to be reunited with my husband in Dufton arriving just in time for a very welcome ice-cream.

I had made a start on the Nuttalls outside the Lake District and had emerged unscathed. I looked over the Nuttalls list often wondering whether I really had the staying power to finish another list whilst, at the same time discovering some little gems on the walks to bag Wainwright's Outlying Fells. Would my feet last out? Was I really capable of finding my way over mountains that I had never even heard of, let alone seen? Not one to let a challenge beat me; I was determined to give it a go.

Chapter 28.
Peat hags and boot sucking bogs

Whilst walking the Wainwrights, I had occasionally come back with muddy boots and wet socks and had come across ankle turning peat on The Nab. However, most of the time, unless I had ventured off the regular paths, I would meet nothing worse than undulating sphagnum moss which ensured I tested my waterproof boots to the max, but didn't cause much of a problem. Reading about the Nuttalls, I realised that if I was to complete this list, I would meet much more testing terrain.

I started to read about peat hags and groughs and call up pictures on google and in books. Peat hags are tall mushrooms of peat above land which has been cut away or eroded and the groughs are the channels which run between these. Some of the images I found didn't look exactly inviting; the depth of the groughs meant that as I walked along these channels, the hags would be above head height. Of course, I had heard of the infamous quagmires on Kinder Scout, famous for the mass trespass of 1932, and realised that this was on my Nuttall list along with other mountains in The Peak District. Even Alfred Wainwright had been victim to boot sucking peat, getting completely stuck in the bog near the summit of Black Hill and having to be pulled out by a friend and a passing National Park Warden

Other problem areas seemed to be in Northumberland and on other North Pennine fells. It turned out that the peat I had met on Murton Fell and The Nab were nothing compared to those I would meet if I were to complete my Nuttall challenge. Wainwright had been lucky to be pulled out of the bog by a walking companion and someone with experience of the dangerous conditions. I was doing this challenge alone. There were many times when I had been on great expanses of moorland without another walker in sight. I had to put my fears to the back of my mind and trust that with common sense and care I could avoid becoming a victim of the bleak and desolate landscapes that I was desperate to conquer.

Oh well! It had to be done. I would tackle the six mountains in Northumberland on another holiday during the year following our visit to Nenthead.

Peter and I had visited Kielder Reservoir with our daughters on our Northumberland holidays so we knew that there were places we could visit and enjoy on my non-walking days. With this in mind we booked a lovely cottage in Otterburn.

Before my foray into the Northumberland bogs, I managed to bag some closer Nuttalls and outlying Wainwrights. I also experienced a miracle find on one of these walks.

On the Twelfth of July 2014, I set out on a very hot Saturday to climb another Yorkshire Nuttall, Knoutberry Haw. This walk started with a lovely stroll by the River Rawthey and with the sunlight dancing on the water, I took quite a few pictures. However, after photographing the waterfalls which were beautiful, though not as full as they might have been as we had had a long spell of dry weather, I put my camera away in order to climb up some rough ground to a clearer path above the falls. The wider river here was a haven for minibeasts and dragonflies circled the water, their iridescent wings, mesmerising in this lonely landscape. One particularly large dragonfly hovered over a small pool on the path, its shimmering wings catching the sunlight. It almost seemed to be demanding that I take its picture. I reached down for my camera; it wasn't there.

It was a fairly new acquisition and I was enjoying using it, pleased by the images I had captured, so I decided to retrace my steps. I was sure that it wouldn't be too far away. I had deliberately chosen a bright purple model so that it would stand out if I dropped it. I made my way back down the steep bank to where I had captured pictures of the waterfalls. In spite of a good search, I could find no glint of the metallic violet casing. I had my lunch, while trying to decide what to do. Whilst packing my sandwich box away, I realised that I had drunk well over half my water and had only done a small portion of the walk. I decided that after one last search, I would abort the walk and return to my car. I drove home feeling dejected; I had not bagged any fells and had lost my camera and with it the photos that I had enjoyed taking as I had made my way along the river.

It was coming up to my birthday so I used some birthday money from my Mum to order a new camera as soon as I got home and planned my return trip to try to successfully reach the summit of Knoutberry Haw. My chance came five days later when I had a teaching-free day. I made good progress at the beginning of the walk as I knew the route. I reached the river above the waterfalls in no time and as I spotted the large dancing dragonflies again; I looked down towards the river and there, at the side of the path, almost camouflaged against the glorious flowers was my purple camera; hanging from a thistle of the same colour. I picked it up and although it seemed to be damp, it didn't seem to have suffered too much from five days in the wilds of the Northern Dales. I used my new camera to record the dragonflies and my onward walk, tucking my recovered camera safely in my rucksack. I kept chuckling to myself as I hiked along quite proud of my find. However, they say, 'Pride comes before a fall.' Sure enough, the path soon became non-existent as I made my way across boggy terrain and at one point, as I was singing happily to myself, my boot found a waterlogged hole and I went down like a sack of potatoes. It was a strange fall; I hadn't hurt myself but somehow found myself stuck under my walking poles which had gone sideways into the soft ground. It took me a couple of minutes to extricate myself and squeeze the water out of my socks before completing the rest of the walk without any problems. My camera was fine after a day or two by the radiator and all my photos were fine and yes; I did get a good picture of the dragonflies. Miracles do happen!

Although I had some painful memories of Yarlside in The Howgills, I would have to return to the area to bag the Nuttalls that I hadn't climbed on me first visit. Always up for a challenge, as you may have gathered by now, I decided to undertake a walk that took in all seven of The Howgill Nuttalls in one day. The walk started with a climb up, yes, you have guessed it, Yarlside. It was going to be another long slog to its summit but this time I would be ready for it and it would be out of the way early in the walk. Even though I was feeling stronger and my feet were manageable, the long grassy slope with its false summits didn't seem any easier and it required a few wine gums to get me up there. In fact, it has remained, up to now, my only five wine gum hill! After that first summit, I had a fantastic day's walking; well, I say walking. The final descent back to the start was once again made on my bottom. That's one good thing about the Howgills; you rarely meet other people to challenge your slow progress or your chosen method of descent. Still, I was getting into my stride and was ready for my first visit to the fells of Northumberland.

Eager to repay Peter for agreeing to yet another holiday focused on my peak bagging, we spent the first day of our Nenthead holiday visiting the Keilder Birds of Prey Centre and having a relaxing boat trip across the water. We also researched some good restaurants that we could visit during the week and ate a delicious evening meal at one of these. Sitting at the table, replete from our meal and drinking a glass of good red wine, I did briefly wonder whether a holiday by the Mediterranean on a Greek island might have been a better idea. However, we had done that several times and travelling abroad was becoming more difficult for Peter; the uneven pavements on our last Greek holiday had caused him to come a cropper on more than one occasion. We had even tried going further afield with a holiday in Morocco after my foot operation in 2012, when we had had to holiday later in the year than usual. That holiday was a disaster with unprecedented rain all week and tummy bugs, so British holidays did, on reflection seem to be a good idea for both of us.

The second day dawned bright and clear for my walk up to The Cheviot and Hedgehope Hill. Ominously, my walk instructions had the often-unwelcome tag, 'Wild Walk' at the head of the map. These words, printed in a little blue circle, meant that some of the walk would be done over pathless moorland. I would have been reluctant to set off had the forecast for the day not been good. I had checked my map and knew that I would have to trust my compass for part of the walk. Actually, the day turned out to be wonderful. Even the bogs that I encountered were shining in the sunshine. The heather, which was in full bloom, accompanied my climb up The Cheviot. This mountain is unusual in that its summit doesn't have the spectacular views that you would expect from over two and a half thousand feet.

I had taken lots of photographs on the way up the fell; my eye drawn to the wide skies over rolling hills and valleys and a distant horizon but as I approached the trig point my eyes were forced downwards as I tried to avoid planting my boots in the ever- deepening bogs at the sides of the very welcome paving slabs that lead the way to the top. There were other walkers at the summit but no-one stayed longer than the time taken for a quick photo of the trig point and its surrounding bog. As I descended to Scotsman's Cairn, the wonderful views opened up again and I chose this as a good place to have my lunch and check my map for the ongoing pathless section of my walk. There was no path nor any of the welcome paving slabs that had helped me to my first summit. However, there was a fence line leading in the right direction. This fence was vital in helping me to keep the correct line across the wet black ground. My boots squelched across the peat, making me think to myself of Michael Rosen's wonderful book, 'We're going on a Bear Hunt'.

> 'Uh-uh! Mud! Thick oozy mud. We can't go over it.
> Oh no! We've got to go through it.'

Because it was such a bright day, I didn't mind the cold splashes of mud and water on the backs of my legs and was quite enjoying jumping from one tuft of dry grass or peat to the next. I got through the worst of the bogs and across Comb Fell. Although the onward grassy path was quite heavy with ground water, I could see that work was being done to manage the moorland. Sheets of firm plastic mesh had been laid across the surface of the path presumably to stop erosion from the many boots, like mine, tramping across to bag the mountains and to protect new seeds and moss, being planted to replace the flora that had disappeared along with the peat. Reaching Hedgehope Hill, the views from the huge summit shelter reminded me why I had started my challenge. I could see across to my beloved Lake District, Skiddaw clearly visible in the distance, and to Great Dunn Fell with its white domes glinting in the sunlight. After taking lots of pictures, to help Peter to enjoy the views vicariously on his laptop, I had a pleasant easy walk back to our arranged meeting place. I was under no illusions that I wouldn't always have such a positive experience of conquering peat bogs but I had enjoyed my day.

My next walk on this holiday was an easy and uneventful one to the summit of Windy Gyle but it was an interesting walk as we were less than a month away from the Scottish Referendum on Independence. At one point in the walk, I crossed a stile, at the top of which I had one foot in England and one in Scotland. I did wonder what would happen to that stile if Scotland became a separate country. Would there be border guards or a barbed wire fence to keep the English out?

One of the less attractively named Nuttalls is Bloody Bush Edge. It could be climbed along with Cushat Law if I was prepared to do a seventeen-mile day. It seemed a lot to ask of my feet but Peter urged me to go for it. It would mean that I would have completed all the Nuttalls in Northumberland. Peter dropped me off in Alwinton and, in spite of a couple of wrong turns, I managed this walk better than I had anticipated. The bogs near the summit of Bloodybush Edge were no worse than those on The Cheviot and I was ready for them. What was unusual was the lack of other walkers.

My seventeen miles were done without any company at all. I enjoyed the peace on the long walk back to Alwinton, which was on a clear, gently descending, path. However, in the middle of the day, when I had lost the path and was walking in a fine drizzle, the lack of other walkers was disconcerting and I had to dig deep in order to concentrate on my map and compass as I tried to find my way.

I think times like this have increased my resilience. Maybe, as human beings, we are rarely put in a position where we have to rely on ourselves totally. We can usually check with someone else whether we are on the right path, during a walk like me, or generally in life. I was standing above a huge forest trying to prevent my map from getting soaked, totally alone. I took a bearing from the corner of the forest to where I thought the summit should be and set off. Within ten minute or so I found a muddy path, but a path none-the-less and spotted the white trig point in the distance. It would have been good to share my elation with someone but even so there was a warm feeling of celebration creeping through my body. As if to celebrate with me, the sun came out and I felt a sense of joy that was different from that I feel on the friendly familiar fells of Lakeland. I was in a wild lonely place but as at one with the landscape as I had ever felt.

Chapter 29.
More bogs and romantic rocks

I enjoyed being a lone walker and was becoming more confident about exploring new territory but I did still wish that Peter could share some of my walks. On a walk a couple of months after our holiday I did a short walk that took me up to Bleaklow Head and Higher Shelf Stone in the Peak District which made me think more of Peter and resulted in me taking a picture that would become his Valentine's card the following February.

One of the joys of walking in the Peak district, is seeing the amazing stone formations on the often otherwise bleak moorland. The 'kissing stones' made me smile. These quite ordinary looking rocks, when viewed from a certain angle look like kissing lips. I took some time taking various shots of these to demonstrate to Peter that, even though he couldn't come with me, he was never far from my thoughts. On this walk I took the bogs in my stride, (sometimes literally) and concentrated on taking pictures of the kissing stones and later of the sadder site of the plane wreckage that litters this moorland.

I suppose on this short walk I had learnt some life lessons. Joy is sometimes found in the bleakest of places and that it can be found alongside the sadness that we can often see around us. People had lost their lives in the plane crash and I offered a quick prayer for those who had suffered loss that day and the kissing stones reminded me to make the most of the love of my husband and family for whose support and encouragement I will always be grateful.

Having bagged two of the Nuttalls in the Peak District I decided that I might as well complete the set and climb the notorious Kinder Scout and set out on a fine November day a few weeks after my ascent of Bleaklow Head.

I enjoyed the ascent of Jacob's Ladder to Kinder Downfall and was in good company; there were quite a few walkers out enjoying the late Autumn sunshine. However, I soon left the other walkers behind as I headed into the large peak hags making my way across increasingly boggy ground to reach the summit. I was getting quite used to walking in this type of terrain but it wasn't easy and felt rather disoriented in the deep groughs between the hags which at times towered above my head.

As I was looking at my compass, I took my eyes off my feet just long enough for my right boot to sink, very

Bleaklow Head October 2014

suddenly, up to my calf in a patch of particularly viscous peat. I obviously acted instinctively and tried to lift my foot very quickly out of the black bog that was encasing it. As I tried, without success, I was aware that my left foot was also sinking, albeit more slowly than my right had done. I decided that the time had come to spread my weight to ensure my feet didn't get lodged any more firmly into the black stuff. Without any care as to what I would look like afterwards, I half sat and half lay across the peat. I grasped my right leg and tugged; hoping desperately that I had tied my boot on tightly enough to withstand the opposing pull of the peat. After, what seemed an age, I heard a satisfying squelch followed by a wet popping sound as I recovered my foot.

I shuffled away from the wet patch of peat before getting carefully to my feet and plodding on to bag the summit, find my way out back onto Kinder Edge and down to my car, drinking in the beautiful peachy light of a winter sunset. It had been another adventurous day when disaster had been averted and I could drive back to Leeds smiling and safe.

Chapter 30.
Big changes

2015 proved to be a very busy year. My hiking had to take a back seat to house moves, a hen do, cake making, a wedding and a big change for us as a family.

The early part of the year was taken up with packing up our house in order to move to a bungalow, more suitable for Peter. The home we found also had an attached annex for my Mum, (who was still living on her own in the family cottage), should she need to move near to us sometime in the future, or just for visitors. I had also agreed to make Rebecca and her fiancée, Tom's wedding cake, which I would have to start the minute we moved into our new house in March.

I didn't stop my challenges altogether, of course, and did manage to do some of the walks from Wainwright's Outlying Fells book on odd days when I found myself free.

As soon as the weather allowed, I was off!

I chose fells which weren't too far to drive to and, with my friend Jenny, set out on a crisp February day to climb Finsthwaite Heights. This walk had the wonderful surprise of a beautiful tarn, High Dam, part frozen in the shade but sparkling, fresh and blue in the winter sunshine. We had loved our short winter walk and didn't feel ready to go home so drove on to Grizedale Forest to make the easy climb to Carron Crag summit. The Howgill Fells rolled under a bright blue sky in the distance and close to us, clouds hugged Top O'Selside as though they were protecting the summit from the winter chill with a blanket of thick cotton wool. The smiles on our faces that day were permanently fixed from the moment we left the car in the morning until we arrived back home.

This little walk had reminded me why The Lake District is my favourite place to be; there are treats around every corner. I wanted to walk more from Wainwright's plodder's guide.

A couple of weeks later, Peter drove me over to fells near Windermere and Coniston to bag some of the pretty fells not far from these popular villages. We chose to stay at a cottage in Far Sawrey where Beatrix Potter had once stayed. This wasn't the best cottage for Peter, with low doors and uneven floors but we appreciated its history and the warm reception that greeted us.

In fact, I started walking even before we arrived at the cottage. Peter was able to drop me off as we rolled off the ferry to Hawkshead and I walked over Claife Heights with amazing views over Windermere. As I came down in Far Sawrey, I had missed out the tarns mentioned in Wainwright's book so I popped out early the next morning to put this right. I was so pleased that I did; the wonderful Langdale Pikes seemed to be within touching distance as I approached Wise Een Tarn.

I was on a roll, and the rest of the day saw me walking over the Top O'Selside taking in the tops of Low Light Haw, High Light Haw and, what I totted up was my four hundredth fell, Brockbarrow, which had a lovely trig point overlooking Coniston Water on which to celebrate this milestone. This was a lovely quiet walk and as Peter had driven me to the Lakes on this occasion, we were able to meet up for tea and cake to celebrate. We didn't have any alcohol with our afternoon tea or we might have questioned what we saw as we walked back to the car; in an old red telephone box we were amazed to see goldfish swimming happily around in their unusual home. I know some of these old phone boxes have been re-purposed as local libraries or homes for the welcome defibrillators but this was a new one on us.

On our return to Leeds, all my time was taken up with packing but in the evenings, I would still spend time perusing books and maps and planning my next adventures.

By March, I had done as much as I could to prepare

for the move and was just twiddling my thumbs, waiting to hear from solicitors about final details and completion dates.

When a day of good weather appeared on the mountain forecast, (just a week before we moved, as it happened), I set off to walk two of Wainwright's Walks that I had decided could be joined together; The Wasdale Horseshoe and The Crookdale Horseshoe.

This was a lonely but beautiful walk which made for a good day of peak-bagging. The scenery was very different from the majestic fells and dramatic screes of the other Wasdale. This one was grassy, gentle and had none of the crowds that seem to stream into the South Western Lake District, attracted by it being the possessor of, 'Britain's Favourite View', as well as its highest mountain and deepest lake. In fact, on this walk, I hardly saw a soul all day. At one point in the walk, I was in a relatively unknown Wasdale looking down into another valley with a name that makes the ears of fell-baggers prick up; Borrowdale; but again, this was a quiet grassy valley known only to those of us who head away from the popular routes to follow in the footsteps of the elderly Wainwright. By linking The Wasdale and Crookdale Horseshoes, I had had a very satisfying day's walking that had taken my mind off boxing crockery and sorting books and clothes and all the other things that occupy one's thoughts when relocating. We moved house without incident three days later.

I did manage to do a higher-level walk in April, mainly because I was aware that I still needed to crack all The Nuttalls in the Lake District. I picked a lovely day to do a short steep walk to Grisedale Pike via a route that I hadn't tackled before. Whichever way you climb this mountain you do have to face the fact that you will have to tackle a steep ascent. However, the ascent via Hobcarton End did seem slightly easier than the more usual relentless slog straight up from the car park on the road out of Braithwaite, partly because it started with a walk through the forest which kept me cool as I heated up from the effort of climbing.

As I emerged from the trees I saw a lone tree on hillside, just before the main path to the summit, that had me puzzling. It didn't look a particularly unusual size or shape but I couldn't make out its 'fruits' or leaves until I got nearer when I smiled to myself. What I had been looking at was a small pine tree complete with Christmas decorations; not quite what you expect to see in April on a mountain. The descent over Ladyside Pike was also steep but quickly changed from scree and slate to lovely springy grass which I was able to bounce down quite happily.

Later that month, I did get out into the countryside again but for a very different reason. Rebecca decided on a day in the Yorkshire Dales for her hen do. We didn't go for a hike, but a wet Saturday saw a group of excited girls and two mums; herding sheep, driving tractors, guiding pigs with large boards, welly whanging and egg throwing on a farm in the middle of nowhere. I loved the fact that Rebecca wasn't tempted by the spa days, trips to Spain or evenings of drinking that many hen dos involve. I felt glad that some of my love of the great outdoor had rubbed off on her. We stayed on the farm and after eating a good supper of pulled pork and salads, we played games in a cosy barn and drank Prosecco before falling asleep on three tier bunks to the sounds of the lowing of cattle and baaing of lambs and sheep.

The next two months were taken up with sorting out the new house and getting ready for Rebecca's wedding. I was delighted to discover that I could walk from our new front door, through a ginnel and over fields, to The Chevin a local hill which at 925ft is a decent leg-stretch. Having found this path, I put it to good use a couple of times a week, walking up to a view point, from which I could look towards Skipton and beyond, dreaming of higher mountains and longer walks. At least I could still get some exercise and keep my feet working. By the end of June, the wedding cake was made and my outfit sorted and the family were all excited for July the 4th; the wedding day.

As Mum was in her eighties and didn't like driving far from home, I arranged to collect her from the cottage on the last day of June so that she could stay in the annex and come to the wedding with us on the Saturday. Everything seemed to be going well. I went back to work on the Wednesday, leaving Mum happily settled and Peter at work.

Later that day, everything changed.

Peter arrived home from work to find Mum shuffling about our house on her bottom trying to find some way to stand up. She had fallen and hurt her elbow so badly that she couldn't get herself up. Luckily one of our new neighbours is a retired paramedic. Peter called him over and it was decided that Mum had probably broken her elbow and that they should call an ambulance.

Peter called me and I met Mum in A and E. As she didn't appear to be in too much pain, I don't think she was put as high up in the list as she might have been and it was several hours before she was taken for an x-ray.

Suddenly, the serious nature of her injury became apparent. Her elbow wasn't just broken; it was smashed into several pieces, the radiographer saying that she had never seen such a bad break. Mum was given pain killers and while they put her in a suitable sling, she was given Entonox. This had the hilarious result of making her rather uninhibited and after flirting with the doctor and making rather rude remarks about the size of another lady's backside, I was glad when she had been made comfortable and in the early hours of Thursday morning was admitted ready for an operation to pin her elbow later that day.

I had very little sleep that night. It was three in the morning when I eventually arrived home and in addition to being worried about Mum, I was also concerned about how it would affect the wedding; would I still be able to go? Would Mum get to be at the first wedding of one of her grandchildren? My mind was racing. The next morning, I rang the hospital to find out when Mum would be having her operation only to be told that I could come and get her. It turned out that the surgeon couldn't repair the elbow and Mum would need an artificial joint which he would order and would probably fit the following week.

I collected Mum and settled her into our annex and obviously had to help her with everything, as her arm was protected by a huge foam sleeve and sling. I had a procession of friends sit with Mum while I went over to the wedding venue on the Friday evening to see Rebecca and oversee last minute preparations but had to return home instead of staying with Peter as planned.

The wedding day dawned and I had to get up very

early in order to help Mum dress for the wedding and drive over an hour and a half to the venue for my hair appointment which had been booked for eight-thirty. When Rebecca had first offered me the chance of having my make up professionally done on her special day, I wasn't particularly bothered; after all it was her big day not mine but I was so glad she had gone ahead and booked it. The make-up artist was wonderful and managed to hide the bags under my eyes which meant that I didn't spoil Rebecca's pictures due to my lack of sleep.

After a wonderful day, my sister, who had travelled from her home on The Isle of Wight for the wedding, was able to take Mum back to our house and look after her while I relaxed and enjoyed an evening with family and friends and a quiet night with Peter in a cottage owned by Tom's parents.

Mum went in for her operation on the Tuesday following the wedding.

Although the surgeon was wonderful and did a brilliant job on Mum's elbow it soon became apparent that she would not be able to manage on her own at the cottage. She wouldn't be able to drive again as the new elbow wouldn't be strong enough. As the car had been her lifeline with the cottage being so remote, the decision was made for Mum to leave our lovely family home. Our annex would be permanently occupied much sooner than we had anticipated.

After a few weeks, Mum was more mobile and able to manage without me so I was able to get back to the fells.

I had only a few Nuttalls left to conquer in The Lake District but my feet were getting more painful again so I was determined to climb them as soon as possible.

At the end of July, I set out for the wonderful Langdales to bag a Mountain that I realised I could have bagged some years before when I had visited Cold Pike on my Wainwright round. It hadn't been on my radar then but I wasn't complaining about revisiting this glorious area. Little Stand, is really a fell runners fell and apparently is on the route of the Duddon Fell Race for this breed of super-humans, (of which I am definitely not one).

I climbed Pike O' Blisco and Cold Pike then headed out for my new fell. I can't say that walking to this summit was an unadulterated joy, winding between various knolls and little tarns, especially when walking in the opposite direction meant heading for the glorious Crinkle Crags. However, when I finally reached the summit cairn; the views made the rather uninteresting trudge worthwhile. The slopes fall steeply to Mosedale and the Coniston Fells can be seen in all their glory. I turned reluctantly from the view and headed for the wonderful crinkles.

On approaching Bad Step, I remembered my previous visit when I had climbed it encouraged by Jenny who, watching me at full stretch, had decided that her legs simply weren't long enough to follow. She met me on the top after walking round. I was glad, after walking over to Little Stand, to follow her example; after all, I had conquered the step once.

I did feel sorry for a fellow walker though. I met her and her walking companion as I came down off Crinkle Crags. Aware of sharpening pains in my feet, I had stopped for a little rest and I noticed that she was looking puzzled and consulting her map. I asked if I could help and she replied that she wanted to tackle the Bad Step but couldn't locate it. On looking at her map in order to point it out, I realised that she was looking at the crinkles, upside down. She thought she had only missed it by a few feet rather than the whole of the ridge. She looked rather downcast when she realised that her desire to conquer The Step would have to wait for another day.

I was, at this stage, feeling that I would be unlikely to visit this lovely mountain again. If someone had offered me a lift back to Langdale via stretcher or helicopter, I would have gladly have accepted. It is a good job there are amazing views on The Band as, with every step, it felt like I was walking on glass and that someone had slipped an iron bar into my right boot. The Band is an amazing construction; a path of huge stones carefully placed in many cases by volunteers to prevent erosion to the beautiful countryside by the millions of feet that make the pilgrimage to Crinkle Crags and Bow Fell but for tired feet those stones are unforgiving. Still, as always, as soon as I reached the car, took my boots off and had a cold drink I was able to reflect on another good day's walking, (or hobbling as it was for the last few miles!)

Women say of childbirth that it is easy to forget the pain when you are rewarded with a beautiful baby at the end of it. I think fell walking is like that for me. I often had pain in my feet of such a level that I would squeal as I tried to get out of bed in a morning. However, one look at the view over a soaring mountain range or reaching a hidden summit cairn gave me such joy that I soon forgot the agony I had been in. I think walking solo helped too; if no-one is there to moan to, you just have to get on with it and if 'it' is walking a few miles down a steep path with fire in your boots then so be it.

Chapter 31.
Feisty sheep and scary cows

I have talked in earlier chapters about the wonders of seeing deer, squirrels and birds of prey on my lonely walks but I hadn't really had any problems with wildlife, and cattle and sheep had seemed happily disinterested as I had passed through their fields. Occasionally they would look up from their grass munching or cud chewing to give me a hard stare as if to ask why I was disturbing their peace.

I guess that most of the paths I had walked up to this point were used regularly and people were nothing new to these usually passive creatures.

I wasn't under any illusions though as to the potential dangers of being trampled by cattle and would pass through fields with any animals as quickly as possible, giving them a wide berth.

My next Outlying Fells hike brought me close to one sheep in a way I certainly didn't expect. I should have been warned though, by the great man himself.

The Bannisdale Horseshoe is the last chapter of the Outlying Fells Book and although Wainwright's introduction to this walk didn't inspire confidence, the term 'grassy slog' did suggest it might be gentler on my sore feet than the hard boulders of The Band.

'NOTE VERY WELL INDEED that this is a walk only for the superbly fit. Being pure in heart is not enough. It is the longest walk in this book and a gruelling test for old age pensioners, a marathon the safe accomplishment of which is a merited occasion for ribald rejoicing; while those who perish on the way must be content with the lesser gratification of knowing they died

with their boots on............ It is a slog over grassy prairies a splendid exercise for the leg and a tonic for the ego.'

I had no intention of dying with my boots on and as I wasn't yet an old age pensioner, I decided that I would tackle this hidden horseshoe. I took my Wainwright with me, using it alongside my map for directions. I didn't meet a soul on this rather desolate walk and climbed over Whiteside Pike taking the featureless grass slopes towards Capplebarrow before detouring to bag Todd Fell. Most of the instructions from this point involved following wire fences while my boots squelched easily across soft wet grass. I reached the small tarn which Wainwright says, 'makes a welcome change of scene and is a good place to halt'. I took his advice and had a break. I read the next section of the chapter and consulted my map. This is what I read;

'Skirt it, (the tarn) on the east side and continue, uphill again, by the side of the fence, (here large-mesh wire, a source of danger to horned sheep, disentangle any found trapped by it).'

I chuckled to myself at the thought of the flat capped Wainwright wrestling with a sheep on this lonely moorland.

I set off looking at the wire fence and imagining this scenario when I saw something ahead of me, that I couldn't quite make out from a distance. No! It couldn't be! It was! Yes, as I approached the kerfuffle, I couldn't believe my eyes; a poor ram was indeed tangled in the wide mesh, his beautiful curly horn wrapped around the wire. His hoofs couldn't get any purchase on the soft ground and it was obviously in some distress. It was on the opposite side of the fence to me which was a blessing as I wouldn't have enjoyed being kicked as I went to its aid. I suppose it would have been good to have a photograph as proof of this incident but my first instinct was to follow Wainwright's instructions to disentangle the poor creature. I am still not sure how I did it but using my walking poles I managed to hold the horn still while I guided the wire around its rigid curls. The Ram was not happy but I knew I had to continue until I had won the battle with the fence. Suddenly, the wire pinged free and the scared animal leapt away from me, as though it was I that had caused his predicament. I did feel sorry for him though. As he bounded away from me, he encountered a very muddy bog. Luckily, it wasn't deep and he was soon on his way, trying to regain his dignity as he went.

As it was more than forty years since Wainwright had written the comment about the wide wire fence being a source of danger to horned sheep, I did wonder why it hadn't been replaced with something less hazardous.

I finished the walk without incident and was glad that the sun emerged through the clouds to cheer me over the difficult tussocky grass of Lamb's Pasture which from a distance looked like a gentle grassy mound. Still, it had been an interesting walk and I must admit that it made me feel at one with Wainwright as I had managed to follow all his instructions for this walk to the letter; well apart from partaking in, 'ribald rejoicing'. I was just glad to get home and soak in a warm bath knowing that I had ticked off the longest walk in The Outlying Fells.

Another encounter with sheep on the Shap fells, led to a less than pleasant experience. In fact, as I write this, I realise that this encounter happened on my return to the A6 after the April walk to bag the Crookdale fells. (Which goes to prove the comment about walking being like childbirth; I had put to the back of my memories the incident that I am about to recall!) I had had a peaceful, solitary day and wasn't far from the road when I heard a loud chorus of bleating and baaing. I had never had a problem with sheep, so wasn't worried until I realised that over a hundred animals were making their way toward me at speed from different directions.

I suddenly became very worried. I was now trapped on three sides giving me only one route of escape. I would have to climb over a fence onto the banks of Crookdale Beck which at the point I encountered it, was flowing in a ravine. The ravine wasn't a deep one but it did mean that I had to watch my footing. I never climb fences or walls without good reason and will walk a good way to use a gate or stile, as I know the work that goes into the construction of these barriers necessary to protect livestock. However, on this occasion, I felt that my action was justified to prevent myself being injured by so many animals.

I followed the ravine down towards the road which I could see snaking across the moor some way ahead. The river narrowed and I was able to cross into a pathless field. Relieved to be safe but aware that I was probably trespassing on farmland, I was pleased to see a gate at the far side of the field. I headed for it as quickly as I could, knowing that although I would have to walk on the road back to the car, I would be on a legitimate right of way. As I approached the 'gate', I realised that the metal construction, though obviously made for this purpose, was just propped up in a gap left in a broken wall. I climbed over but then saw a man coming towards me, looking very angry indeed. I tried to explain what had happened and that I had headed for what I thought was a gate. He told me that it wasn't a gate and that I had been trespassing. I apologised, still not sure what I was supposed to do. I was met by a torrent of abuse which would have shocked a navvy. I felt very tearful as he stormed off telling me that he hated f...ing walkers. This is probably the only time that I have been met by anything other than pleasant words from helpful farmers and it was a shock to say the least. Luckily there were some road workers nearby who had heard him shouting at me and gave me some kindly words which were an antidote to the farmer's vitriolic diatribe. I tried to excuse his foul language by thinking that he had probably had a bad day but it had shaken me.

Cows are regularly encountered on approaches to the fells and are usually docile animals but there have been several reports of walkers being attacked by them so I am always wary.

I was to meet some less than friendly bovines on Caermote Hill in 2016. This was only a short walk so I had planned to do another fell later in the day but it wasn't to be. I approached the first gate and as I opened it, I was aware of a herd of cows heading straight for me. I quickly retreated and closed the gate. I chatted to the cows telling them that I wasn't the farmer with their dinner and that I had nothing for them but at this stage I wasn't at all worried as I just assumed that it was a case of mistaken identity. I waited around for about five minutes until the herd dispersed and went back to grazing their patch.

I finally carried on my way hoping to get to the summit without any more problems. I did reach the interesting cairn which has several memorial plaques which I read as I ate my lunch. I started my descent but I gave the cows a wide berth as they had still seemed to be watching me as I made my way to the summit. However, at one point they

The first herd of cows blocking my way to Caermote Hill
July 2016

lined up neatly along one edge and every eye seemed to be on me. It wasn't my imagination. I quickly but calmly followed the route described by Wainwright but walking several metres wide of the path to put more distance between myself and the cows. I was very nervous, with good reason as it turned out. It suddenly dawned on me that more cows were lined up in front of me and were moving to form a circle with the first group. I was surrounded on all sides. They weren't too close but there was no way out of the trap they had me in.

There was no point shouting for help; there was no one around. Luckily, there was a field break running across the diameter of the circle. This took the form of a ditch with hawthorns along its length. There was nothing to do but to climb in amongst the scratchy branches and lower myself into the ditch. I was probably in the ditch for less than ten minutes but it felt like hours.

Eventually the cattle must have decided that I was no longer worth bothering with and gradually wandered off. I climbed out of the ditch and made my way shakily to the first exit from the field that I could see. I wasn't in the right place but it didn't take me long to get back on the right path and make my way back to the car. The relief was immense but I was shivering and shaking as I rung Peter and told him that I was heading home. I felt as exhausted as if I had climbed Scafell Pike. One of my favourite trees is the hawthorn and on this particular day I hadn't another reason to put it at the top of my list.

I am not sure what it was about the cattle in that particular area but when I climbed Clint Crags a year later, my walk to the summit was once again accompanied by the loud braying of a herd of cows who stared at me as I walked past them, at what I judged to be a safe distance. This time they stayed where they were, just making sure that I wasn't going to invade their territory for too long. I didn't hang around to see what would happen if I overstayed my welcome and actually had a pleasant walk back to the car catching sight of two beautiful hares as I walked away from the cattle, vowing that Caermote Hill and Clints Crags would be two fells that I would steer clear of in the future.

Although I was worried by these incidents, I comfort myself with the thought that I have walked past cows, goats, sheep and even pigs hundreds of times without any reason to be concerned. However, I would never take my safety for granted and take signs on farmland seriously. I would also advise anyone to think about what they would do if they encounter problems of the kind I have described and to be vigilant when around livestock. I was very lucky and I don't blame the farmer or the animals for my problems. We are lucky to be allowed to walk freely in our beautiful countryside but must never forget that these are working environments for lots of people and we shouldn't take it for granted that we will always be welcomed with open arms by those who have more right to be there than us.

I encourage all walkers to follow the Countryside Code and earn the respect of people who work the land and let the animals reside there in peace. A gate left open or wall broken may not just be an inconvenience for these hard-working folk but might cause real problems for escaping animals and even risk the life of valuable livestock.

Chapter 32.
Hobbling to my second foot operation

I stuck to grassy walks over outlying fells during the summer of 2015 and my feet coped well but were still far from comfortable, especially when I walked on tarmac or a hard road surface. I was referred to another foot surgeon who was willing to have a go at straightening my hammer toe and bunion in my right foot. This was the same operation that I had had three years earlier on my left foot which, unfortunately, hadn't been a total success; hence the reason I had chosen a different hospital and surgeon to do the operation. I was told that this particular specialist was very strict with his patients but had good results, so I was hopeful. I was also very happy that the operation would be done in winter when I usually have a break from walking anyway and that as the weather improved through the spring, my mobility would hopefully improve at the same time.

As the operation date got nearer, I got worried that, if it wasn't a success, I might have to say goodbye to mountain walking as a hobby. Rather than making me depressed, this thought spurred me on to at least complete something. I decided that I would finish all the Nuttalls in the Lake District before I was admitted to hospital. I only had three left, Looking Stead on Pillar and Middleboot Knotts and Round How near Scafell Pike. All these mountains could be climbed from Wasdale.

I realised that I could also climb Scafell Pike from Wasdale, a route which I had never used and in doing that

I would also be climbing solo to the highest point in England; another first. I tried to book into Wasdale Youth Hostel but they were fully booked for the weekend in October that I chose for the walk so I booked into Eskdale Youth Hostel where I had stayed on my first hostelling holiday over forty years earlier.

As I didn't want to leave Mum for too long, I only booked one night, so the Scafell walk would be done after the long drive from Leeds.

I parked the car at Wasdale and got out to the most beautiful sight. The sky was blue and the air clear and cold; a perfect day. I set off to climb to the summit of England feeling strong and excited. There were a good number of people on the path but not so many that it felt crowded. As we got higher, white clouds gathered and swirled around but it never felt cold or damp. Before I knew it, I was at the trig point celebrating with others who had made the ascent. For many of my fellow hikers, this was enough; they had achieved what they had come to do and I was happy for them but for me, I still had some more peaks to climb.

As I looked around me; I could see that the white cloud was covering all but the highest summits around me. I could see the domed top of Great Gable peeping though the cotton wool cloud and I caught the beautiful scene with my camera. What I didn't know at the time was that a friend was on Great Gable at that very same moment looking at Scafell Pike.

I left the summit, heading for Broad Crag. There was a steep descent into the cloud before climbing out again. At the low part of the saddle between the two mountains, a strange honking sound had me looking skyward; suddenly a skein of geese burst through the clouds and arrowed its way across the col. It was a very strange sight at three thousand feet. I climbed to Broad Crag summit following this quickly with Ill Crag, where I was once again walking above the cloud which was lovely.

Unfortunately, I descended back into swirling mist which wasn't quite so good and I had a few moments of doubt while I looked for the path to climb Great End. Luckily, it wasn't too long before I reached the summit cairn of that particular mountain, once again in sunshine. Although I didn't 'need' this fell; it gave me a good point of reference to take a bearing for Round How. As I left all other walkers to bag this fell, the sun went in and the mist was swirling so that Round How kept coming and going from view as I approached it. I had been walking for most of the day on hard rough rocks but the ground around this Nuttall was, in contrast, grassy and even in some places quite boggy. This was quite a relief for my feet but it was strange to be in such totally different conditions so close to the barren rocks only five hundred feet above me. I was in an eerie bleak gully on my own and was glad to make my way back down to the corridor route to reach the final summit of the day Middleboot Knotts. I had been close to this peak before but hadn't realised that it was a fell in its own right. There were amazing views into the exciting Piers Gill but I was very pleased that the mist had cleared by this time as it is known as a notorious blackspot where many walkers have sadly lost their lives.

I had only one more Nuttall to bag in The Lake District, (or so I thought) and in spite of the familiar pain in my feet, I made my way back to my car, stopping regularly to rest and to take pictures of the sun dropping quickly in Wastwater, feeling very content. It was dark as I made my way into The Eskdale Valley and it seemed to take an age to reach the hostel but I was welcomed warmly and as I had phoned ahead to tell them that I would be late, my meal had been kept warm for me.

I had had a satisfying day and was looking forward to climbing Looking Stead the next morning.

Although I awoke to a day more overcast than the previous one, I was able to reach Looking Stead summit without any problems but with my feet as they were, I decided not to push myself too far and resisted the pull of Pillar, making my way down by the route of ascent. I drove back to Leeds believing that I had completed all the Nuttalls in The Lake District and tried to wait patiently for my operation.

My operation went ahead as planned just before Christmas. The surgeon, this time was much stricter about what I could and could not do to ensure a successful outcome. As I still unclimbed fells, I followed his instructions to the letter. This meant keeping my foot raised at all times for two weeks. I had permission only to visit the toilet and make myself a drink if no one else was around to do it. I even ordered our Christmas Dinner from Marks and Spencer's. Luckily, with the weather and busyness of the season, I wouldn't have been heading for the hills anyway.

My pins and stitches were removed and the operation declared a success and I slowly got back onto two feet.

My right foot certainly looked better than the left had looked after the operation in 2012 but I still couldn't contemplate walking. When I went back to the hospital for check-ups, the surgeon decided to do another x-ray of my feet. He found that, as he put it, there was a lot going on in my feet and any further operations would probably be too risky. He decided that I needed to see a rheumatologist to see if they could do anything as there was definitely evidence of arthritis that needed to be investigated.

Having been referred to a rheumatologist a few years earlier who had dismissively said that I had a raised perception of pain and should do more walking, (How much more could I do?), I was doubtful that they would find any answers this time. However, I agreed to the referral and waited for an appointment. In the meantime, the surgeon who had done my operation decided that I would benefit from steroid injections into the neuromas around my toes!

I gradually built up my walking, round local parks and nature reserves but didn't feel confident until March to undertake anything more testing than these gentle strolls. Besides, I had been kept busy looking after Mum, who early in the new year had had a hip replacement. At one point I was taking her for her physiotherapy appointments in a taxi while still wearing a protective boot on my foot. The physios must have been a bit confused when we walked in.

I did accept the 'kind offer' of the steroid injections. I wasn't looking forward to it but sometimes you have to suffer to do what you love. The first injection was as bad as I expected. I did squeal quite loudly at one point. When I apologised, the doctor told me that I had done well. He said, 'You only squealed, I usually get kicked when I do that.'

The effect was almost immediate. I had a huge reduction in my pain level and so went in for my second treatment with a more positive attitude. That one didn't hurt quite as much but didn't have such an amazing result. However, I was poised to walk again when I got the chance.

As the weather improved, the hills started their siren call and I felt my feet itching to be on the fells again. I was wary about venturing too far and my first outing was over the beautiful, wind-swept Ilkley Moor. I think I did walk, 'baht 'at', but can't quite remember. I was off again and out came my lists once more.

I thought I had finished the Lakeland Nuttalls, but still had some Outlying Fells to climb.

Peter was happy to see me eager to be out again and we spent a lovely day at Pooley Bridge at the Northern End of Ullswater and I managed to climb two small fells: Dunmallard and Heugscar Hills without any problems. So, a week later I was out again tackling a slightly longer walk in the remote valley of Swindale. This time, the fells were a bit higher and I really began to feel that I was doing some real walking. The area is lonely and remote and in places quite boggy, but the gentle terrain would not be too taxing for my feet. This walk took in five summits so was to make a good dent in the list of Outlying Fells.

Wainwright says of this walk: -

'*The round of summits described in this chapter is a worthwhile expedition on a clear day, not so much for the views, which are extensive but dreary and uninspiring, as for the exhilaration of new territory, solace of solitude, and beneficial exercise.*'

I think Wainwright must have done this walk on a dull day, because I thought the views were anything but dreary, but I was definitely as exhilarated as he had been. The healing hills were working their magic.

I was ready at last to move to a new area to climb more Nuttalls.

Chapter 33.
Exploring New Territory

I had two areas of England left to complete my Nuttall journey. Peter and I had already booked a holiday in Devon for July so that I could climb the two mountains in that county; High Willhays and Yes Tor. Our holiday had to be carefully planned as these mountains are on military land near Okehampton and there are restrictions on the days that there is open access to them and I didn't want to risk getting shot at or arrested.

The other area was The North Pennines. I had left this until last for a couple of reasons. Firstly, I thought that it was too far to drive to do a day's walking and the other reason was that many of the walks on Go4awalk had, 'Wild Walk' on their instructions. This meant that I would be walking not only in unknown territory but also on terrain that may be pathless and that I would be relying on my compass and map reading skills.

I settled down with my maps and laptop and started to investigate The North Pennines. I knew that my feet weren't ready for rocky terrain and that grass and bogs would be easier on them. I also knew that I needed a walk with a very clear starting point. A walk from Burnhope Reservoir in County Durham seemed to fit the bill. I was very surprised to find out that the drive there would take me less time than driving to the Lake District. I chose a bright spring day with a good mountain forecast. The walk was going to be fourteen miles which would be a real test. I arrived at the reservoir without any trouble and was delighted to find that there was even a public toilet which most walkers appreciate as a real luxury.

Wainwright's comment on my previous walk about the solace of solitude, could equally be applied to this one. I didn't meet a soul but had the company of sheep early in the walk and the birdsong gave me a pleasant soundtrack to accompany my squelching boots. This was a good walk for navigating through peat bogs as, although paths were few and far between, there was a fence which ran as straight as an arrow between some summits and which I could track back to when I had found the safest way through and round the hags and groughs. The first mountain of the day was probably the hardest to navigate as it took a long detour away from the fence line and the bogs were relentless. I was certainly glad of my gaiters.

I was very happy to get back to the reservoir with five Nuttalls under my belt and an improvement in my confidence in tackling this lonely, barren moorland. I was enjoying being back in the hills and my mood was lifting.

I was back at work and Mum was still needing my care so there weren't a lot of days to hike. I was still needing to use insoles and dressings on my feet as they were still tender but it was a small price to pay and I could now look forward to completing my challenge.

I mixed up my walking for the next couple of months whenever I got the chance, steadily working through both my lists.

Just before Peter and I headed for 'sunny' Devon, I got my choose and book letter for the promised investigations into my arthritis. I decided to opt for an appointment at Harrogate Hospital. I hadn't been there before and I liked the idea that it was smaller than Leeds Teaching Hospitals. I made my choice and waited.

Peter and I were really looking forward to our holiday in Devon. Gillian, my sister was going to be looking after mum so I could really relax. I would only be hiking on one day as both Nuttalls could be done in one walk. We would have lots of time to enjoy the Devon sunshine and hoped to visit Cornwall, sit on some beautiful beaches and explore the Lost Gardens of Helligan.

Indeed, our journey down promised much. I even bought a sun hat and new sunglasses on the way down as it was so hot. Sadly, that was our only sunny day. We woke up to rain on the first day of our holiday and it never stopped.

I did manage to bag the required Nuttalls but it was a bit of a trudge in drizzle rather than the easy walk, in strong summer sun, that I had expected. We did make the most of our week visiting some great National Trust properties and I took a magical but wet walk in Tintagel but it wasn't quite the summer holiday we had hoped for.

I had had one trip onto MOD land and I still had another one to do when we returned home. There are several differing about the rules for accessing Mickle Fell.

However, I assumed that if I downloaded the list of access weekends and went on one of those, I would be fine. I still don't know whether what I did was allowed but I didn't get shot or arrested when I hiked to the summits of Burton fell and Mickle Fell.

Burton Fell is a curious fell in that it has a long narrow top without any evidence of a rise in the ground that would denote a summit. It has a trig point shaped cairn which is clearly not the top, then the trig point which is really battered is hidden in a shelter but the ground rises beyond that too. Luckily, I met a fellow walker up there. I had a grid reference for the summit cairn and the gentleman I met had a GPS, so together we were able to locate the few stones that assured us that we had bagged this Nuttall. The gentleman walked down in the opposite direction from me and I was left alone to walk towards

Mickle Fell which looked magnificent in the sunshine surrounded by high wispy clouds and blue sky. Unlike Burton Fell, there was a huge cairn which I had no problem locating and I made my way down feeling relieved that I wouldn't have to enter military land again. (Well, that is what I thought at this stage anyway.)

I climbed when I could over the next couple of months bagging more Nuttalls and Wainwright's Outlying Fells without incident; my feet holding up but still far from comfortable. I finally got my appointment for a consultation about my aches and pains at the hospital of my choice.

The Rheumatology Department at Harrogate Hospital was a breath of fresh air.

Here were people who listened and who cared about fact that the pain in my feet was limiting my love of walking. My wonderful consultant embarked on weeks of trials on different drugs which she thought might help. She monitored my condition and responses to the drugs she was giving me. Even though there were some improvements, she still wasn't happy with the swelling and pain in my joints and was curious about the, 'points of pain', which I was reporting on the ends of my bones in many places on my body. After a few months, she kindly called on the advice of another consultant who asked me about these odd pains which feel like new bruises. I pointed one or two out to him and he immediately found several more without me having to direct him. From my reactions and the answers that he got on questioning me further, he diagnosed me with having Psoriatic Type Arthritis in addition the Osteoarthritis which was responding to treatment.

This hadn't been picked up as I have never suffered from the skin condition, psoriasis, which usually accompanies this condition. A different treatment was suggested which was to give me a new lease of life. I was put on an immunosuppressant and things gradually started to improve. I was excited to think that I may be able to enjoy pain-free walking once the treatment built up in my system.

It is amazing; just having someone who understood my need to complete my challenges in spite of my age and health problems gave me a new confidence and a determination to go into 2017 to do exactly that.

Chapter 34.
New Nuttalls

Several friends knew about my ambitions and the lists that I was completing. One of them came up to me one day and said, 'I see that you have a new mountain to climb.' I wasn't sure what she meant until she showed me the story that she had seen.

The Ordinance Survey Mapping Agency were remeasuring the English Mountains with new and more accurate equipment. I was going to have to keep an eye on this story if I wasn't to miss any summits above two thousand feet. Reading The Nuttalls' book, I noted that over the years several mountains had been added to, and removed from, the list. My job was to complete the list that was current at the time of me finishing. The new fell wasn't too far from Gragareth, a mountain that I had enjoyed some years previously. In fact, I realised that that mountain could be seen from the new one, Calf Top near Barbon. This had been measured at exactly two thousand feet, therefore meeting the definition of a mountain.

I enjoyed climbing this fell with its far-reaching views and it is one I might have missed without this remeasuring.

Two more fells that were added to the list were on Warcop Military Land. Yes, I would have to go back to the firing grounds that I thought I had seen the back of. Long Fell and Tinside Rigg had been reclassified as mountains and needed to be climbed so out came the access timetable once more.

I set off on a dull but clear spring day to bag these two rogue mountains. It was more obvious than on my previous visit that I was on military land. It was the first time on a walk that I had seen artillery shells and bunkers. However, the walk itself wasn't difficult and I really enjoyed it. I suppose I felt like I had been given permission to trespass on land that few people get to see. Route finding wasn't as bad I thought it would be, even though it had been termed a wild walk. I was careful to steer clear of the debris that lay around, just in case I should trip over something that would cause more than a dent in my shin should it prove to be live.

Where there was no obvious path, I was able to use my map and compass for finding the route back over another summit, Roman Fell. At nearly one thousand, nine hundred and fifty feet with a large cairn and shelter on its highest point, this seemed a more worthy objective that the other two slightly higher fells whose tops were only marked by cairns comprising half a dozen stones. There was no one else around and although the feeling of solitude was disturbed somewhat by the reminders of the land's usual purpose, the views were wonderful. The Yorkshire Dales, Lake District, Howgills and North

Pennine Moors were all visible and I felt very privileged to be the only one enjoying those particular views that day.

Chapter 35.
More lonely North Pennine walks

The promise of contrasting views, are what draw me back to The Lake District time and time again; a sparkling tarn appearing at the top of a hard climb, a tower of oppressive rock above you as you walk along a ledge, a beautiful valley opening up below you as you turn a corner. However, the Lake District isn't the only place in England that can take your breath away with is glories.

I was finding out that the 'bleak' moors of The North Pennines, while often boggy and devoid of beauty on the ground, held their own wonders. I really was at one with the landscape on many of the fells. Indeed, in completing all thirty-four of the mountains in this area, I only saw five people in total. Soon after my walk on Warcop, I took on a walk to bag Binks Moss. I realised as I parked up that I had been to this area before. I had visited High Force Waterfall one day when we were staying in Alston on a family holiday. I was so tempted to visit the falls before I started walking but I resisted and set off away from people in the car-park, (about to set off for a gentle stroll to see this amazing sight), and away from the falls, saving the spectacle for later in the day. Yes; the ground was wet and the paths were far from clear but as I plodded to the top of Green Fell, on the way to the Nuttall summit of Bink's Moss, I stopped for a breather and was blown away by the panorama that stretched out below me. I took this in with my whole being before capturing it on my camera to show my husband later. The wind blew hard but it wasn't cold and I was enjoying its cooling touch after the climb, the earthy, fecund smell, that accompanied the boggy ground, tickled my nostrils as my eyes took in what I was seeing. Being alone with these sights made me feel as special as if I had been given a solo tour of the National Art Gallery. This was why I pushed though pain, trudged with wet feet, and got up at crack of dawn to drive to remote destinations. I wouldn't have wanted to be anywhere else that day.

I almost hugged myself with delight and I walked on to the summit of Binks Moss. As I reached the top of the wide moorland, my smile turned to a chuckle. The top was marked in a way particular appropriate to the conditions underfoot. There were a couple of stones acting as a cairn but these were hidden under two sticks supporting two upturned wellies. I wondered whether this particular pair had been abandoned mid-walk; if so, how did their owner make his way down the hill? If not, why had someone bothered to carry a dilapidated pair of wellington boots up the mountain just to decorate a summit that few people would see. Anyway, I was grateful for the marker and for the moment of fun on what was already a wonderful day.

I had no company on this walk but wasn't missing it; I waved at a skein of geese as they flew in front of me, the point of their arrow showing me the ongoing route. I lost height, making my way back to The River Tees though crags and twisted, spikey juniper trees. I soon found myself beside the wide fast flowing river and soon heard the roar that told me that I was reaching the magnificent High Force; what an end to a walk. I approached the glorious cataract with my camera snapping and a smile on my face. Luckily, most of the crowds had gone and I sat by the falls taking pictures of the torrent in front of me and a beautiful robin sitting next to me on a rock totally unperturbed by the force of nature being unleashed only yards away. I had had a perfect walk and still had time to drive to Nenthead, where Peter and I had spent a lovely holiday and lace up my boots again for another quiet hour popping up and down Dodd, another North Pennine Nuttall. I was losing count of the number of Dodds I had climbed on the quest to complete The Wainwright's and The Nuttall's but this was an easy one and worth climbing before I drove home.

Chapter 36.
A walker or a mountaineer?

It is strange that, although I had been solo walking for several years and had always got down safely, I still looked with awe at walk reports on-line and listened avidly to tales of adventurous walkers, without realising that I was becoming one of them. In my mind, I was just a walker that followed other people's instructions and could use a compass when called upon.

The North Pennine Nuttalls had started to give me more of a sense of adventure than other walks had done. I couldn't call on a passing walker for confirmation of my route or rely on clearly marked paths repaired by, 'Fix the Fells' as I usually could in The Lake District. In fact, it was one rather uninspiring walk in this area that suddenly made me realise that I had become a hiker with not just an internal map of the fells but an intuition that the last few years had begun to instil in me.

I tackled Chapel Fell Top on a day which started cloudy, but promised to be sunny later in the day. It wasn't cold but as I walked from St. John's Chapel, it wasn't long before I was walking into cloud. I was looking for a gully to follow through the peat hags but with the damp humid air swirling around and black peat beneath my feet, I couldn't see anything resembling a gully that I could follow with any confidence. As I had done several times in this area I slid and squelched my way up hill; after all, if you are heading for a summit then the only way is up!

I was following my compass through the mist as best I could and the ground seemed to level out. I guessed that the top couldn't be far away. I wandered through channels of mud, climbing onto hags to see if I could make out any higher ground. All of a sudden, I got a feeling that I had over shot the highest point. I didn't appear to be losing height but I just felt in my bones that the summit was somewhere behind me. I turned round, scouring the cloud covered land around me as I went. After only a few yards, I spotted a wonderful landmark, one that has given this book its name; another pile of stones!

A friend had once asked me why I bothered climbing all these mountains when all that was at the top was a pile of stones. Peak baggers will understand though. The joy of seeing these man-made wonders can be out of all proportion to their size. They mean for us, success.

That particular day on Chapel Fell Top, I had a feeling of satisfaction and a sudden realisation that I was a true mountain hiker. No, I may not have been up the giants in The Alps, or tackled Kilimanjaro or Everest Base Camp but I had an instinct that had led me to this particular point without any GPS or phone map. From the summit I was able to follow the channel that had eluded me earlier and head for my next summit without difficulty. The mist never did lift and as the sun showed no sign of breaking though, I called it a day and made my way back to St. John's Chapel but I did so with a new found confidence that I could now truly say that I was a mountain climber. I thought that this revelation would come while scrambling up Jack's Rake or scaling Pillar via the high-level route, not standing in black peat in the mist on the barren North Pennine Moors.

I didn't know the North Pennines like I knew the Lake District so I often came upon surprising sights that I hadn't noticed on the map, as I was usually concentrating only on finding paths to the summits.

I had set off on a bright cold January Day to climb Cold Fell in Geltsdale, (a dale I had never heard of until I researched The Nuttalls.) I enjoyed the climb to the summit and reached it without any problems. However, I must have missed the path on the descent and ended up on some tussocky grass trying to make a very steep descent. I was a bit concerned as I could see a building below me and a transit van parked outside.

I hoped I wasn't trespassing on someone's land but the building gave me somewhere to head for and the presence of the van meant that there was a road in the vicinity. I made a far from graceful decent on my backside using my poles to prevent any dangerous slide which might have taken me down over the rough ground faster than I had intended. I did have to climb over a barbed wire fence at the bottom of the slope which definitely told me that I wasn't where I should have been. I saw someone approaching the van and was a bit concerned that he would be coming my way to reproach me for my actions. To my surprise, he got into the driver's seat and drove off either unaware or unconcerned. With the obstacle of the van removed, I could see the building more clearly. It was an RSPB Visitors' Centre. By the time I got there, it was closed but it was an amazing find in this remote corner of the North Pennines. Not only could I pinpoint my position on the map, I was also treated to my first ever sighting of a gathering of red polls; a pretty bird that I have been lucky enough to spot since in the Western Lake District, which welcomed me down from the fell with a chattering chorus.

I had got down to the car with an hour or so left to bag another fell before the light faded. Maybe my unorthodox route back had saved time. There was a direct path shown on the map to the summit of Renwick Fell (or Thack Moor) from the village with the same name. The whole walk would be four miles; just about doable before dark.

I nearly came a cropper on the way to Renwick. I turned a sharp corner in a small hamlet and hit a patch of black ice. I struggled to control the steering as my car ran up a bank and almost hit an icy stone wall. Luckily, the car came to a stop just before the wall and I climbed out to assess the damage. Surprisingly, there didn't seem to be any so I gingerly got back into the driver's seat and carefully reversed down the bank. I was able to drive off without any problem and the frozen ground meant that I had hardly made any mark on the grass.

A bit shaken, I reached the village and looked at the fell ahead of me. It was bathed in red light from the setting sun and I knew that my return journey might be in darkness. The path looked good though so I check the batteries in my head-torch and set off, passing a lovely country church on my way. Unusually, I did meet a fellow walker on my way up this fell but he was on his way down. He did reassure me though, that the path was clear. I reached and photographed the snowy trig point before turning round and heading down. It was getting dark and I was just thinking about donning my head-torch when I saw the beautiful lights of the church below, guiding me down. As I got nearer, I was aware of the glorious sound of church bells ringing out in the cold crisp air. The descent from this fell was joyful as the sound got louder and the lights got brighter to welcome me back to my car. I was beginning to enjoy these lonely fells and their wonderful surprises.

Although I wasn't walking on familiar territory, I was loving my Nuttall Challenge as much as I had The Wainwright's, but for different reasons. The rugged rocky scrambles were absent as I reached the end of this challenge but with deserted stretches of moorland and miles of walking without seeing a soul, I had time to ponder and find peace in a life which was becoming increasingly busy and uncertain.

Following Mum's recovery from her hip operation, things settled down at home. However, she decided that having me make her meals as I had done while she was incapacitated, was something that she didn't want to relinquish so she would potter through from the annex to join us every day for her meal at exactly five thirty. Peter's walking was getting more problematic so he was given a desk job and different hours at work and could help less at home and I was still teaching three or four days a week.

It may be difficult to understand why I pushed myself

so hard to complete the two ongoing challenges, while life itself was enough of a challenge.

I think I would have found it hard to say, 'I just need to go for a walk', but because I had specific fells to climb and there was an end in sight, I somehow felt empowered to 'go for it!' No matter how tired I felt or how many things were on my 'To Do' list, as I drove off to another unknown area with my rucksack and walking poles, I breathed out the tension so that from the minute I pulled my boots on, nothing had to occupy my mind other than following my route and drinking in the sights and sounds of the wild open moorland.

Chapter 37.
Two more endings and the elephant in the room

I wasn't particularly planning for any celebratory ending to my Nuttall or Wainwright Outlying Fells challenges; it felt a bit self-indulgent to expect anyone else to be particularly interested in these lesser-known achievements. I did have to finish somewhere though and started to check carefully through my lists so that I didn't have a rogue summit to climb after declaring that my tasks were complete.

I just had a few Nuttalls left in the North Pennines at the beginning of 2017 most of which would inevitably involve a lot of mud unless I was going to wait until later in the summer but I had got used to mud, so decided to go for it. However, in March I did manage to avoid what had been described by several people as some of the worst bogs they had encountered by climbing two fells and then driving to a different start point for the third rather than risk getting stuck.

I climbed Grey Crag and Tom Smith's Stone Top from Gilderdale Bridge, not far from Alston. Grey Crag had a well- constructed cain and a trig point built into a wall corner at its summit which was a really welcome sight on these often-lonely fells. I walked on to Tom Smith's Stone Top which, in marked contrast, hardly had anything to mark its top. As I hadn't brought the snorkel and waders recommended by a fellow walker who had walked from here to Black Fell, I decided to retrace my steps to the car. I didn't do this as well as I hoped as at one point, I took my eye off my compass, saw a wall and followed it thinking that it was the one I had followed up the fell. I reached a river where I wasn't expecting one and took a while to find my position on the map. I realised where I had gone wrong and spent a few minutes wandering up-stream to find a crossing narrow enough to be safe and once over was able to make my way down the road and my car; not quite coming out where I expected to but thankfully only a couple of hundred yards away.

I then drove to the iconic Hartside Café which sadly was burnt down just a year later. Although I knew that I hadn't much daylight left I was going to be following a fence to the summit of Black Fell and back from near the café, so I felt fine about completing my third Nuttall of the day. It was a good decision. The ground was very wet but it was only a mile or so to the summit. The light was fading but I still had distant views towards the Northern Fells of the Lake District. Skiddaw and Blencathra were topped with a covering of snow and the setting sun was turning the white to orange.

It was a lovely sight to distract me from my feet which in spite of waterproof boots and gaiters were getting wetter and wetter. I didn't hang around at the summit and was soon back at the car. I sat on a wall outside the café and could hardly lift my feet to unlace my boots. Having done so, I pulled off my socks and wrung so much water out of them that I could probably have filled my water bottle twice over!! My dry socks and trainers felt wonderful. As I drove away from my parking spot the sky turned a glorious red. In fact, it was such a wonderful sunset that I pulled in at the first opportunity and got out of the car to capture the sky streaked with vivid reds and oranges. I had nearly finished The Nuttalls, bogs and all.

During April 2017, I was able to bag most of the remaining mountains in the North Pennines. I also reached a milestone after yet another disorienting hike over peat hags trying to avoid sink holes. On this occasion I couldn't follow a direct compass line but could clearly see a significant plateau in the right direction over the hags, which I could aim for. Luckily, my intuition was right and I reached my five hundredth summit since I had started 'bagging' on my way to the highest fifty Wainwrights, over ten years earlier. Meldon Hill is marked by a derelict cairn and the view makes the difficult walking worthwhile. This walk also included a return visit to High Cup Nick and this wonderful landmark made the onward route much easier as I knew where I was heading and my eagerness to see it again added a spring to my step.

Suddenly my Nuttall journey was reaching its conclusion.

I had one to go and I hoped I would have company on Killhope Law which to be my last. (Or was it?)

I chose Killhope Law as I knew I could walk there and

back from Allenhead on a clear path. Allenhead was somewhere Peter and I had been with the girls during one of our Northumbrian holidays and it had a good pub for Peter to wait in so that he could share the celebrations. Looking at the map I did wonder during the planning stage whether Peter would be able to join me on this final fell as Carriers' Way, the route I would take, looked like a good enough track for an all-terrain mobility vehicle to tackle but this wasn't the case and I didn't really know where I could hire one from; it was just a bit of dream. Hannah decided that she would like to join me on the completion of another challenge as did a friend who also loves hill walking, (even though she has no interest in peak-bagging.)

My Godson, Thomas, and his girlfriend, Caroline, also wanted to be part of the celebrations but preferred to keep Peter company in the pub rather than do any walking.

I chose a date in June when I thought we might have good weather; well, it wasn't raining!

In fact, the day was misty and very windy. Hannah, Corinne and I battled our way through the wind to reach a summit, unfortunately, hidden in the mist until the last minute. I had envisaged heading for the forty- foot pole, that I had seen in photographs and the Nuttall's book, planted in the summit cairn in bright sunshine. I thought that the huge marker would be a fitting end to my challenge. In fact, the pole was lying rather forlornly on its side in a muddy pool. Corinne and Hannah laughed as I made my way through the puddle for the obligatory photograph.

As if to celebrate with us, the sun came out and we had a lovely descent, with the wind at our backs and curlews wheeling around us in the clearing sky. It was a delightful end to our short walk. I was given congratulatory hugs and we settled down to a tasty meal before heading home to register my success on The Nuttall's website and on Go4awalk.

I was quite excited to register my completion of yet another challenge and the next day I put together some photographs to submit to Go4awalk together with an email of thanks for the help that their website had been. I received a reply which planted a seed of doubt and another challenge in my mind.

'*Congratulations and well done. There is just the small elephant in the room of Pillar Rock. I won't say anything if you don't but it does need to be climbed if you want to truly, hand on heart, with all honesty, claim to have actually bagged all the English Nuttalls.*'

I honestly hadn't thought that I would have to climb Pillar Rock as part of my challenge, as reaching its summit would involve a roped climb. I surmised that, as this was well out of my comfort zone, it would be the same for other walkers and we wouldn't be expected to climb it. I had been over The Shamrock Traverse on my way to Pillar and thought that would suffice.

I decided to contact The Nuttalls. I discovered that walkers can indeed be added to the list of completers without tackling Pillar Rock. I was therefore, duly registered as a completer of The English Nuttalls with NPR, (Not Pillar Rock), in brackets. I could now concentrate on finishing the Wainwright Outlying Fells.

Chapter 38.
Completing the Outlying Fells

I only had a few odd fells left, no long horseshoe walks and nothing really to get the adrenalin going. Inevitably, these last few were in the far West of the Lake District. The days were getting longer so I did have time to drive over to the Western side of The Lakes for a day trip. I wasn't particularly looking forward to climbing Ponsonby Fell as Wainwright's comments didn't exactly whet my appetite.

'There are no fells not worth climbing, but Ponsonby Fell is very nearly in this category.... The only justification for spending time on it is the splendid approach through Blengdale Forest, which, unlike most modern plantations, retains much of its natural deciduous woodland and has many well-spaced mature conifers lining its riverside road. Blengdale makes the climb worthwhile, but only just.'

On a beautiful August day, I drove to Gosforth near Wasdale which, if I hadn't been determined to climb this uninspiring fell, could have drawn me to something more exciting, which from Wainwright's comment wouldn't have been difficult. However, Ponsonby Fell had to be ticked off so I pressed on. As I made my way into Blengdale Forest some amazing views opened up before me. These were a wonderful surprise and all the better for being unexpected. There had been some recent logging and the sweet pine sap oozing from the neatly cut trunks and the clover scattered through the grass was obviously attracting the minibeasts.

Colourful peacock butterflies and red admirals had

settled on the logs looking like spatters of bright paint all along the path and the sound of buzzing from bees and wasps provided a soundtrack to my walk. I made my way through this forest of delights and dropped down ready to cross The River Blenge. In spite of the heat of this particular, there must have been a lot of recent rain and without taking off my boots and paddling across, there was no way I was going to reach the other bank. Undeterred, I backtracked and decided to take a path deeper into the forest that I had seen on the map and which seemed to lead to a bridge further up the river. There was a forestry gate across the entrance to the path and I wasn't sure whether the onward route was barred to me or just to unauthorised vehicles. As luck would have it, there was an occupied caravan near the gate. A forestry worker, on his day off, came out of the caravan as I passed and assured me that I would have no problems, especially as a lone walker who didn't look as though I was going to cause any problems to the trees or logging equipment.

I continued on this delightful walk until I left the forest and started the climb to the summit. Here, for a hundred yards or so, I agreed with Wainwright.

'*... aim for the top of the fell through tall rushes. The ascent is slow and tedious, and the summit is attained with a conviction that nobody has ever been there before: it is surprising to find this impression contradicted by a small heap of stones that some anonymous enthusiastic cairn builder has laboured to gather.*'

The grass was long, tussocky and pathless so the going uphill wasn't easy but this was soon forgotten as I reached the brow of the hill.

Here I definitely had a different experience to the great

fell walker who continues;

'Nor is the view of Lakeland much reward, being severely restricted by nearby Lank Rigg, Haycock and Seatallan. There is little cause to linger.'

I can only assume that Wainwright had summitted Ponsonby Fell on a dull day or in a bad mood as he omitted to mention that from this wonderful vantage point the Ennerdale and Wasdale Fells opened up in a glorious panorama. I could even make out Scafell and Scafell Pike and the wonderful pass of Mickledore between them. I certainly did linger and took plenty of photographs of the views before descending to Gosforth through fields and another wood, having thoroughly enjoyed a walk that I hadn't had high hopes for. This had illustrated again the joy of The Lake District; good weather and clear views can turn any walk into a stroll of beauty.

As my last few fells were also in the Western Lake District, Peter and I planned a holiday in this area. We found holiday-let in Silecroft for a week at the beginning of September. We hadn't stayed quite so close to the coast before and we enjoyed watching a glorious sunset over the Irish Sea on our first evening after a relaxing evening meal in the local pub.

The following day we drove over the wonderful Birker Fell Road which we had used many times to visit our favourite Bed and Breakfast in Eskdale. Hesk Fell dominates this road and I could probably have climbed it many times. However, because we were usually on our way to Forest How or on our way home, I didn't usually pass it when I was dressed for walking. This particular day, I was ready and Peter dropped me at the Woodend Road from where I walked to Wainwright's 'prominent tree' and from there reached the summit of Hesk fell and the further summit of The Pike with no problems and was down in good time to meet Peter who had been down into Eskdale for his lunch. I was able to spend a few minutes visiting the tiny church at Ulpha which was somewhere else that we had driven past over the years.

It was lovely to see The Pike, the fell that I had just climbed framed in the entrance arch to this simple place of worship.

As I looked at the views of the Scafell range from the rolling grassy Hesk Fell, I couldn't help being thankful that I had completed the 214 Wainwright Fells before doing the Outlying fells. I could only imagine my frustration had I been looking out on those giants wishing that I had climbed them. Knowing I had set foot on them all, made the views from the summits of the Outliers all the sweeter. Mind you, I still needed the help of Wainwright's Pictorial Guides and my maps to know what I was looking at. There are some fells which are instantly recognisable; The Langdale Pikes, Grisedale Pike and Great Gable can be pointed out without any doubt but it would be a few years before I was more confident in my ability to describe the view to fellow walkers and to recognise familiar fells from unfamiliar angles.

There were just two fells left Flat Fell and Cold Fell. I climbed these a couple of days after the Hesk Fell walk. They were as exciting as their names suggest. I summitted them both as quick up and down walks while Peter waited in the car doing a sudoku. I did Flat Fell first and actually set off up the wrong fell from the forest car park but soon recognised that I was on the Coast-to-Coast route to Dent Fell. As I hadn't planned to do the whole circular walk, I retraced my steps and took the path directly to Flat Fell summit.

I made my way down to the car and we drove to The Cold Fell Road so that I could complete The Outlying Fells with a quick walk up Cold Fell. Apart from visiting the pretty Matty Benn's Bridge at Wainwright's suggestion, this fell is probably, in my humble opinion, the least interesting of the outlying fells but the fact that it was my last, did keep my spirits high as I searched for the slight rise in the ground that Wainwright talks about. I did actually find a stone marking what appeared to be the highest spot, photographed it and made my way back to Peter. That night we drove over to Eskdale to have a celebratory meal to mark the end of my challenge.

Chapter 39.
The elephant rears its head (or trunk!)

Before we had left for our holiday, Mum had given me a hundred pounds 'ice cream money'. I had tucked it away in a drawer as I had an idea that had been brewing since June and I certainly wouldn't be spending a hundred pounds on ice cream. As you may have guessed by now, I didn't like the idea that I had brackets after my name on the Nuttall's list. I looked back at the email that Mike, one of the editors from *go4awalk*, had sent me. He had actually admitted that he hadn't done Pillar Rock either and that if I decided to do it and found someone to guide me on the climb, he wouldn't mind joining me and sharing the cost.

I started reading about Pillar Rock.

Wainwright gives three pages to the rock in book seven of his pictorial guides, 'The Western Fells'. His comments leave one in no doubt that he did not feel that it was something that the 'ordinary' fell walker should tackle.

'*To walkers whose experience is limited to easy scrambling on rough ground, Pillar Rock is positively out of bounds. Don't even try to get a foothold on it. The climbing guides mention easy routes (the Old West and the Slab and Notch) but these are NOT easy for a walker who is not a climber and lead into dangerous situations. Remember the stretcher box.*'

(The stretcher box refers to one which is at the end of the High-Level Route to Pillar.)

I then turned to John and Anne Nuttall's book in which they describe their impressions of Pillar Rock.

'*On the northern flank of Pillar overlooking the dense packed conifers of Ennerdale is a massive, magnificent tower of rock, rising some five hundred feet from the hillside on its northern edge and cut off from Pillar by a vertical sided chasm above which the summit of the rock is tantalisingly out of reach.*'

They then go on to describe how they roped up to climb to the summit by the Slab and Notch route and descend the same way. Although they didn't make it sound difficult, when he had suggested they return to climb by the Old West route, Anne did say to John that she had had enough and that she wasn't a climber.

Well, I wasn't a climber but I didn't like the brackets.

I decided to start by looking for someone who might take a fifty-eight-year-old novice on her first ever rock climb. Someone had suggested a chap called Alan Pearson, who ran a business called Climb-in-the-Lakes. I contacted him to see whether he would take on the challenge or whether he would think that I was too much of a liability.

I was surprised, when I received an email from him saying that he would be happy to take me up Pillar Rock and that it was something he had done for people doing the Nuttalls before. I contacted Mike who decided to join me. We set a date; the challenge was on!

From the minute I knew that I was going to tackle the climb, I started having very vivid dreams. I had a recurring dream in which I was on a rope, climbing to the summit, when the whole rock would break away from the hillside and plunge into the sea below. I do realise that Ennerdale isn't anywhere near the sea but those are the sort of anomalies that appear in dreams. In my more lucid thoughts during the day time, I did wonder occasionally about my sanity!

In the meantime, I decided to look for some unclimbed fells in The Lakes and found a couple of Dewey's, (Fells between one thousand, six hundred and fifty and two thousand feet), that I hadn't visited while climbing the Wainwrights or The Nuttalls.

I found a walk above the beautiful Buttermere that would take me to some of my favourite fells while bagging some that I had bypassed. It was a good day, if slightly cool for August, just a few weeks before my ascent of Pillar Rock.

I set off from Buttermere to Red Pike on a route I knew well. I soon worked up a thirst on the climb and I was glad I had filled my three-litre water bladder, even though it was heavy. The heather was coming into bloom and gave the reflection in Bleaberry Tarn a pinkish hue. I was enjoying the scenery and making good progress when I met a walker who seemed to be struggling on the steep path after the tarn.

I offered him some water and wine gums but he insisted that he was okay so I walked on. The loose red rock near the top of the aptly named pike can pose a problem for nervous walkers. I had learnt from experience that keeping going at a good pace is the best way to stop the, 'one step forward two steps back', problem that tentative walkers encounter. I was climbing well when I reached a lady on all fours who seemed to be making very little progress. She asked how on earth I was simply walking up when she couldn't even stand up without sliding backwards. I did point out that I was using walking poles and that I had done that climb on two occasions before. I offered to lend her one of my poles and a hand. She was very grateful and together we made our way to the top quite easily. However, she turned when she heard someone shouting from below.

It transpired that the man that I had encountered earlier was her husband and that she had two sons who had gone ahead. Her husband was shouting for her to throw him a bottle of water. I enquired what water they had and it turned out that they had a two-litre coke bottle between the four of them. I don't think the gentleman could have been thinking clearly. I had to stop her from doing as he asked as the bottle would have cracked easily on the red stones and their precious water would have evaporated in seconds or drained into the dusty ground.

We reached her sons and together they sat to wait for her husband to join them. I was torn about whether to go down to help him or to continue with my walk. In the end I shouted down to encourage him to keep going and to ask passing walkers if they had a drink that he could have a sip of. He hadn't far to climb to reach his family and they were happy for me to go on with my walk. I spoke to the sons, who were in their mid-teens, suggesting that they stayed on the summit, when their dad reached them, to have something to eat and drink and a rest before descending back to Buttermere. They had intended doing a full day's walk and I am sure the boys would have been fine but I felt both parents had probably reached their limit. I suggested that they took the path down towards Scale Force where they could enjoy the beauty of the waterfall and walk back to Buttermere, satisfied that they had climbed a fell that many walkers find to be one of the tougher ascents in the Lake District. I doubt that Red Pike is on few people's 'favourite fells' lists. However, it does lead to fantastic ridge walks so I really don't mind it but I doubt that that the family I met would return in a hurry.

I continued on my way, making my way over High Stile and High Crag before dropping down the steep Gamlin End, sliding and slipping down the dry, loose scree. I climbed to the summit of Seat, a Dewey, which I couldn't remember climbing previously and on this glorious day, I didn't want to miss anything. I was walking well and felt that I had plenty of energy as I climbed towards Wainwright's favourite fell, Haystacks. I also had to go in search of Green Crag, a second Dewey. As there are quite a few crags around Haystacks, I wandered around using my map and compass to locate the minor top of Green Crag. After scrambling to the top of that and taking a picture of the small cairn on the heather clad summit, I made my way to the banks of Innominate Tarn where I intended to sit for a while. I spotted a nice flat rock to use as a seat and headed for it. The next minute my foot must have caught on a rougher rock and I found myself pitching forward and I went down on my left knee like a sack of potatoes. I squealed

On Pillar Rock September 2017

with the sharp pain that ran up and down my leg and slowly got up and hobbled my way to my chosen seat. I felt nauseous with the pain and was aware of wetness tracking down my leg from my knee; this wasn't going to be pretty.

I rolled up my trouser leg and using tissues and antiseptic wipes, cleaned myself up as best I could. There was a small hole in my knee cap from which blood was bubbling steadily but the little flap of skin was still attached and I thought that if I stuck it down well with a couple of plasters, I would be fine. I stood up after patching myself up and tried to put my weight on my leg. It hurt but it was going to be okay to get me down the steady path to Buttermere. I tentatively made my way down towards the lake path trying to distract myself with glimpses of one of the most beautiful views in the Lake District. After a few hundred yards, I was aware that the plasters hadn't stopped the bleeding but I really didn't want to keep stopping so I carried on and hobbling, made my way back to the Fish Inn. Once inside, I asked if they had a first aider who could check on my injury but the barman said that they were only allowed to treat injuries that had been caused in the pub itself but told me where the Minor Injuries Unit was in Keswick.

I had a much-needed cup of tea before dragging myself to my car and heading, as suggested, for a medical opinion on whether my knee needed a stitch or not. I was aware that the bruising was making my knee stiff but I wasn't in too much pain by this stage. I drove into the drive of the small clinic when I realised that it was in darkness apart from its security lights which lit up the parking area. I was too late; the minor injuries unit was closed. However, the car park gave me good light and a private place to examine my injury. I zipped off the lower part of my walking trousers, which were a bit red and sticky anyway. I peeled off the saturated plasters and cleaned up the area with an antiseptic wipe and as if by magic the dramatic looking injury shrunk to a small and insignificant looking hole. I felt a bit silly but the amount of blood had led me to believe that it was a lot worse than it was. I dressed the area with a clean dressing and drove home.

My knee was very painful and swollen the next day but certainly didn't need any medical intervention. The only thing that concerned me was, would it affect my climb?

Even a couple of weeks after this incident, although the swelling had gone down and the bruising was fading, the area where the sharp rock had pierced the skin was still very sore. The day for, 'The Climb' got nearer and I tried to practise taking my weight on my knee to see whether I would be able to use it if needed. I knew by this time that it wasn't going to stop me but it was far from comfortable. I needed to find something to pad up my knee that wouldn't prevent me being able to bend and stretch it fully. A bandage was out as that would restrict my movement and a plaster wouldn't really be enough. I found the answer in my foot 'equipment'. With all my foot problems, I had acquired various protective pads. A cushion, meant for the ball of the foot, fitted neatly over the sore spot and could be secured with small pieces of tape. I could stop worrying about my knee; (though I couldn't stop the worrying dreams in which I dropped to my death, in various terrifying scenarios).

I booked a night at Wasdale Youth Hostel on the shores of Wastwater and checked arrangements with Alan and Mike and before I knew it, I was off for yet another adventure in my peak bagging life.

I didn't want to leave Mum for too long as she was needing more help than she had previously, so I didn't arrive at the hostel until early evening. I had a pasta dinner and went for a walk down to the lakeside just as the setting sun started to paint the dramatic screes a soft orange and the mountains, that surround the lake, were topped with small white clouds in a deep blue sky. Everything looked promising for the following morning and although I was still nervous, I was excited for the challenge and was looking forward to getting rid of the brackets. I spoke to several other hostellers who were a bit taken aback when they asked what I was planning for the next day. I don't think they could quite believe that this fifty-eight-year-old lady, on her own, was preparing to be roped up to climb a rock that some of them were going to be pleased to view from a safe distance on their way to Pillar.

The plan was to meet Alan and Mike at Wasdale Head at nine so I had my breakfast, fixed my foot cushion to my knee, put my orthotics in my boots, packed my rucksack and drove down the side of the lake. I was pleased to see plenty blue sky and a fluffy white cloud over Yewbarrow but was concerned to see heavier, greyer clouds gathering over the screes which looked much more formidable than they had the previous evening. I was hoping that the grey clouds would give way to blue sky but it could easily be the other way round.

I managed to find Mike after recognising his camper van and also having seen his picture on go4awalk. We made our way to the meeting place. We did make the mistake of approaching a random stranger, thinking that it was our instructor, as he was in the right place at the right time. I was concerned that he was asking us questions about the fells around Wasdale. Thankfully, as the stranger disappeared in search of a loo, Alan Pearson came round the corner, looking much more professional and organised.

Alan did say that the forecast wasn't good and that he had tried to contact us the day before to see if we still wanted to climb. Unfortunately, (or fortunately as it turned out), as both of us were in Wasdale the night before with no phone coverage he had been unable to reach us.

We decided that we would go for it and set off on the four mile walk to the base of Pillar Rock. The higher we got, the more the weather started to close in. We were soon walking in drizzle and were climbing into heavy cloud. We were all in good spirits though and I was surprised to find that I was keeping up well with the men. The rocks were slippery and there was one point at which Alan decided to rope us together so that we didn't have an accident before we even reached the Robinson Cairn, (a memorial to the pioneering rock climber and founding member of the Fell and Rock-Climbing Club, John Wilson Robinson) and the point at which we dropped down, from the main path to Pillar, to the start of our climb. Before long we were taking off our rucksack and donning helmets and harnesses. I looked at the black mass looming through the mist and asked Alan if he thought we'd would be able to climb it in the poor conditions. His reply gave me a real lift.

'Christine, what you don't realise is that I have been assessing your capabilities for the last four miles. If I didn't think you could succeed, we would have turned back before now.'

In the next hour I would complete my first ever rock climb and know that I had truly finished the English Nuttalls; with no brackets.

Alan explained carefully what he wanted us to do. He would go first placing nuts or stoppers in the rocks and securing the ropes, I would go next and Mike would follow, removing the stoppers as he passed them. We were off!

There was one point where my leg didn't seem quite long enough to reach the slim ledge that I was trying to put it on and my arms weren't strong enough to pull me up so I put aside my dignity and asked Mike to give me a shove. After that little blip, we climbed up to The Slab. This was the first part of the climb done and Alan told us to take a breather while he secured the next part of the climb, The Notch.

Soon we were climbing again. I really enjoyed this second part of the climb and at one point, Alan even said that I was climbing like a real climber; I was loving it. As I reached Alan, just before a small ledge he met me with the words; 'Off you go, the summit is just over there.' I knelt on the ridge; not even thinking about my injured knee and pushed myself to my feet on a surprisingly grassy summit and made my way to the cairn, though one wasn't really needed, as the top was not in any doubt!

Mike joined me and Alan took our celebration picture, at which point he noticed that, although I had a huge grin on my face, I was shivering uncontrollably. I guess the adrenalin, that I had needed to get me up there, had left my body and the cold wet air was doing its best to get into every gap in my clothing. Alan pulled a body warmer out of his rucksack for me to put on over my own waterproof which was very welcome. There was no point staying too long at the summit as we had no view and still had a four mile walk back to Wasdale to do. We had to get down. My nerves came back ten-fold. I was not looking forward to the abseil. This time, Mike was sent over the edge first.

Although, I couldn't see him, it was a relief to hear him shout that he was down. Then it was my turn. Leaning backwards off a rock when you can't see where you are going fights against every bit of common sense and my body resisted for what seemed like ages. Once I was almost horizonal and my feet were walking down the rock I was almost enjoying the experience until all of a sudden, my feet kicked out and found nothing. I had obviously reached an overhang. I started to spin while Alan continued to lower me slowly down into Jordon Gap. I did start to walk down rock again and it wasn't long before I saw Mike and the ground. I was down.

Alan joined us and together we made our way back to our rucksacks and packed away our helmets and other equipment. As before, we were roped up for crossing the wet slabs on our way back to the main path but other than that we just had the long trudge back to Wasdale Head. I found this descent more difficult than it should have been as I was walking on jelly legs and the distance seemed to have doubled. Before long though, we were walking into Wasdale Head. After a quick debrief and shaking Alan's hand and thanking him for getting us safely down, Mike and I headed into the Inn for a well-earned bowl of soup and cup of tea. The celebratory drinks would have to wait as we both had long drives home and knew it would take every bit of concentration we could muster after our exciting but exhausting, strength-sapping day.

Chapter 40.
What next?

Every time I finish a challenge, I convince myself that I will just walk for fun and repeat my favourite walks without any particular aim. Again, I tried finding new local walking routes to satisfy my itchy feet. When I did go up to The Lakes, I continued working my way through the Dewey's that I hadn't climbed which usually involved walking on familiar fells as well.

There were other matters to take up my time at the end of 2017. One of these was the happy news that Peter and I were going to become Grandparents at the end of December or beginning of January. Rebecca and Tom had delivered the news on Peter's birthday in June when they gave him a card to 'Grandpa'. We were delighted of course and my knitting needles were soon working overtime.

The other, more distressing news, was that Mum was diagnosed with Alzheimer's. We had noticed her doing odd things such as trying to warm her nighty in the microwave; burning a hole in it in the process. She would also have to be directed back home by neighbours when she went for a short walk around the block. We were glad that she was living with us as it would have been worrying if she had been living on her own in the cottage. Day to day there wasn't a lot of change in mum's routine but we were reluctant to leave her alone for long. We had the smoke alarms checked and bought a small fire extinguisher and fire blanket in case of repeat microwave incidents. (There were several but luckily none had serious consequences.)

The desk job that Peter had been given because of his deteriorating mobility, meant that he had to start work at five thirty in the morning, Monday to Friday. I wasn't going to be able to head for the hills early in the morning as Mum would be too confused to be starting the day on her own and I couldn't really leave her for long anyway. My walks would therefore have to be restricted to weekends when Peter could keep an eye on her and there would be people to call on if he needed help. I was also still trying to work when I could, usually doing two or three days a week supply work. Luckily, Mum got up early and I could settle her before work. Mum was usually fine watching morning television and was okay to get her own lunch before Peter got home mid-afternoon.

With less time to walk, I decided that would have to look the Lancashire Hills and The Peak District. I reckoned that in just over an hour from home, I could be tying up my boots and taking in a new summit or two before driving back in time to cook dinner.

I was surprised to find out just how many fells there were in Lancashire that I hadn't climbed. I hoped 2018 would see me summiting several of these.

Before that though, we spent some time getting to know our new Grandson, Bertie. After keeping Rebecca waiting over Christmas and New year, he finally put in an appearance on the third of January. His delayed entrance meant that my sister was able to come and look after Mum while Peter, Hannah and I headed off to Berkhamsted to meet him.

On our return to Leeds, we only had a couple of weeks before Mum was admitted to hospital with an infection and I was going backwards and forward visiting and sorting things out for her coming home. I was also working three days a week, so even fells close by were put to the back of my mind. I had completed my challenges and I had more than enough to occupy my time.

I did buy a new Wainwright book to research new routes for when I was able to get out. 'Walks on the Howgill Fells', included some of the walks that I had done while climbing The Nuttalls but I didn't know this area very well.

I found a short walk that could be done from the A6, near the Shap Fells that I had visited while doing the Outlying Fells. I managed to take a day in February to get my walking boots on. This was only a short walk and I was conscious of not being away from Mum for too long. Peter was very good with her but neither of them was very steady on their feet and I always worried when I was away.

I did have a chance to breathe the pure air of Lakeland and spend some quality time listening only to bird song and the squelch and crunch of my boots as they walked alternately over soft ground that had been exposed to the winter sun and patches of frosted earth that its rays hadn't reached. I did manage to bag three new summits, Whinfell Beacon, Mabbin Crag and Ashtead Fell, all over fifteen hundred feet, from which I looked longingly across to the snow-covered peaks in the distance, reminding myself that my favourite fells weren't going anywhere and would be waiting for me when I got the chance to return.

I realised, after this brief outing, that I still needed to walk, even if getting out was not going to be easy. Hiking up often lonely fells was a way of recharging my batteries. Far from being a selfish pursuit; walking meant that I returned home less jaded and more able to cope. Peter got a happier wife and Mum got a daughter who was refreshed and more able to face the challenges of being her carer.

Chapter 41.
A disastrous day

In April, I headed for The Howgills again, looking forward to another day of recharging my batteries and bagging some new fells, unaware that I was going to have one of my hardest walking days ever.

As I expected, I was alone as I walked along Carlin Gill, enclosed by steep banks which looked quite forbidding. Although it was a bright, clear day, I didn't feel comfortable being trapped in the valley where it was cool and quite dark. I was looking forward to getting onto the tops. The steep climb up to my first fell of Docker Knott looked unpleasant and was largely pathless. I wasn't even cheered by the waterfall, 'The Spout', which normally would have had me taking photographs from every angle.

I hauled myself to the fell's summit but there was no spring in my step. I decided that I would be fine once I had warmed up and plodded off over to the descent that had to be done before another grassy climb to the summit of Simon's Seat. This was climbed at an even slower pace than the previous fell. It was a case of ten steps up and then rest before another ten could be contemplated. My legs felt like lead; something was wrong.

I felt a bit light-headed and nauseous by the time I reached the few stones marking the top. I decided that the two steep climbs had drained my resources and that I needed to have an early lunch. I took a break and refuelled. To save my legs, I descended to Langdale Beck on my bottom. I felt marginally better and reached for my camera to record the view of Hazelgill Knott, my next fell, before I started yet another gruelling climb; it wasn't there! My map case, in which I was carrying; a GPS, (I had been given one for my birthday the previous year but it had rarely been used), my camera, and a map of the route; had come open on my bumpy bottom ride down the steep slope. My camera must have jumped out without me noticing. Under normal circumstances, I would have retraced my steps, however, looking at the pathless slope, I couldn't face it. I had the older camera, (the one I had found hanging from a thistle), in my rucksack so retrieved that and slogged up to the summit.

I was nearly in tears by the time I reached the top. I was feeling dreadful and there wasn't a soul around. I was worried. I really did feel alone and lonely; not a feeling I was used to. I managed to get a signal on my phone and called Peter to tell him that I was struggling and that I was going to retrace my route back to the car. This was a shorter option than going on. (Besides, I had done all the remaining fells on the route before.) He did ask if I needed Mountain Rescue but I declined. I could still walk and I knew where I was. I would just take my time and keep in touch when I could.

How I dragged myself up and down the steep slopes I had just tackled, I have no idea. Even the hope that at least I might find my camera, came to nothing. I had only walked about three miles but it felt like thirty in the bleak terrain on leaden legs. All the descents were done in the same manner as the one from Simon's Seat and I did take a couple of pictures to remind me of what I had achieved, that is until I reached 'The Spout' again. Feeling ill had obviously stopped me from learning a lesson from the previous downhill disaster. This time, it wasn't only a camera I had lost but my GPS as well. I had never felt so miserable on a walk; ever.

I walked along what I hoped was Carlin Gill. (At this point, I wasn't even sure whether I had followed my route back correctly.) Following the river earlier in the day, I had crossed from bank to bank to keep to the driest path, now I didn't care. My feet were wet, but that was the least of my worries. Miraculously, I did reach the car. Less than six miles of walking had taken me more than seven hours and I had nothing to show for it; no photographs of glorious views or happy memories of a rare day out.

I drove home, had a much-needed bath and curled up in bed after settling Mum for the night, while trying to be upbeat about my day so as not to worry her.

I felt better when I woke the next day and, apart from my lost devices, was no worse for my experience. I spoke to Hannah about the difficulties I had had. Apparently, she had felt the same and hadn't even been able to make it round the supermarket before giving up. We guessed that we must both have been suffering from some sort of virus that had laid us low. Hannah was amazed that I had been able to get back to my car and I was cheered by the fact that I had got myself out of trouble once again.

I had thought that maybe the stress of caring for Mum, working, worrying about Peter and wanting to be near Rebecca and Bertie had taken its toll and that my walking might have to be shelved for a while. Even so, I had no desire to return to Carlin Gill and its surrounding peaks just to take photographs to prove that I had been there!

Chapter 42.
Familiar mountains again

It was over a month until I got my next proper walk and it couldn't have been more of a contrast to the disastrous day which I had put firmly behind me. I had wanted to see the Rannerdale Bluebells for a while but had never been in the right place at the right time.

Mum seemed quite stable and Peter felt able, with Hannah close by, to look after her while Jenny, another walking friend, and I made an early start one Saturday in May and headed for Crummock Water. We resisted the temptation to glimpse the bluebells before our walk and headed steeply up Whiteside, where Jenny, who had spent her childhood in Norfolk, heard a familiar accent as we chatted to a chap near the summit. She enjoyed a few minutes chatting about places they both knew and sharing tales of a place that I had only been once on holiday.

After the initial climb, the rest of the Coledale Round was a delight, the panorama, in every direction, taking our breath away. I couldn't believe that I had climbed everything I could see. Some horrid flying insects, stopped us eating our sandwiches at the head of the horseshoe but this was a minor irritation in a perfect day. As we descended Wandope and Whiteless Pike, we decided against climbing Rannerdale Knotts so that we could walk along the valley behind that lovely little fell and hopefully get our first view of the bluebells away from the crowds. Suddenly, we saw a blue field. We had been on bluebell walks before but they were usually displayed under trees in a forest. Here, they were out in the open, turning this usually green landscape into a magical sapphire carpet.

Any aches and pains and tired legs were forgotten as we took in the wonderful sight. Even if you have seen pictures, nothing prepares you for the mesmerising glory and sweet scent of these beautiful flowers. We couldn't stop smiling; what a wonderful day we had had. We treated ourselves to a Lakeland Ice Cream before heading home, refreshed and very, very happy. I was more determined than ever to replicate that feeling as often as I could even though I had more demands on my time than ever.

Chapter 43.
One summit, two naked men!

After the wonderful walk with Jenny, I did start to limit my outings to walks that could be done within an hour of home. Settle was somewhere that I hadn't explored and it was exactly one hour from our front door to the main car park so In June when I had the chance, I headed off for my first solo walk for a while.

I had found a walk on go4awalk that promised to visit, 'The prettiest waterfall in the Dales.' It sounded lovely. I pulled up in Settle and whilst sorting out my rucksack for the day I realised that I had left my lunch back at home. It was lucky that I was in a village with a famous sandwich shop and café; Ye Olde Naked Man Café and Bakery. I popped in a bought a tasty looking cheese and tomato roll wrapped in a paper bag with the name cheerfully emblazoned on the front. The name tickled me and I walked up the steep hill out of Settle grinning to myself, wondering who the naked man had been.

I was soon in Limestone country and although I hadn't planned to climb a fell that day, I spotted a ladder stile which seemed to lead to a path up onto the white

Attermire Scar. If there was a summit to be bagged, I wanted to bag it. The summit area was a beautiful surprise. The chalk white rocks were scattered across a wide grassy area surmounted with a trig point and a neat cairn from which I had far reaching views of The Three Peaks of Yorkshire and just across the valley I could spot the impressive entrance to Victoria Cave the next point of interest on my walk.

The sun came out and the blue sky was streaked with high white clouds while on the ground I spotted rich blue speedwell flowers amongst the white rocks mirroring the colours above. I made my way back to the lower path so pleased that I had managed to add an unexpected peak to my walk. I then climbed towards Victoria Cave, passing quite a few cows with calves close to the path but the grass must have been tasty as they carried on munching and paid me very little attention for which I was grateful. There were a few small caves to explore reaching back into the hillside. I didn't go far in but they were fascinating and I easily could imagine settling down in one to escape a heavy downpour had I been unlucky enough to have been caught in one. There was no danger of that; this day was perfect and the sun was warm on my back. As I ventured into the last of the caves, I could see something moving at the back. A sensible ewe had taken her twin lambs out of the hot sun and they were obviously just waking up after a nap and nudging mum for a feed. I left them in peace and walked on.

My next objective was Catrigg Foss but even on the way there was more to see. Amidst this limestone landscape were huge erratic boulders left by glaciers in the last ice age.

I reached the signed footpath which wound down through a cool woodland to a beautiful waterfall, hidden until the last minute. It dropped into a clear pool which looked so inviting. As I started to photograph the pretty fall, probably not as dramatic as it would have been after a lot of rain but attractive none-the-less, I realised that I was not alone. An elderly gentleman was sitting on a rock at the far edge of the pool. He had removed his outer clothes and was obviously getting ready for a dip. He asked me if I wanted to join him but I declined. He asked if I minded him going in which I thought was odd and replied that he should go ahead. What I hadn't realised was that he intended to skinny dip! In the next moment, I was aware that I was in the company of my second naked man of the day. I was a bit surprised but not offended. However, I did decide not to hang around and was careful where I pointed my camera.

The final part of this interesting walk took my mind off the unexpected sight at Catrigg Force as I wound my way back to Settle. The path along-side a railway track was lined with wild flowers; buttercups, coltsfoot plants, foxgloves, purple and white phlox and tall wild daisies added to the joys of this walk but there was more to come. The route back took me on a history tour through the remains of the Craven Limeworks, there were the remains of kilns and tunnel entrances with information boards to teach me more about what I was seeing.

I had enjoyed the most glorious day and one to be remembered for so many highlights and for the unexpected encounter with not one but two naked men!

Chapter 44.
On the Lancashire fells

As Mum's health deteriorated, I decided that I needed some help. I was introduced to Carers Leeds, who were to help us in so many ways over the next couple of years. Initially though, they helped me to apply for Carer's allowance and Attendance Allowance for Mum. Although I was still working, it was becoming more difficult to leave the house in a morning with Mum tearily begging me not to go. When I went to the staffroom at break times and for my lunch, I would look at my phone and find it crammed with missed calls from home. When I got home, Mum denied having phoned me at all and assured me that she had been fine but it was becoming impossible to give of my best both at work and home.

I was put in touch with a local day centre, Memory Lane, which became a lifeline. On her first visit to this wonderful home from home, Mum decided she was happy to stay for lunch and joined in some of the activities. They, unsurprisingly, didn't have a lot of vacancies. However, they did have a Friday slot and Mum could start going straight away. This meant that, once she was settled at the centre, I had a day to myself. A member of staff from Memory Lane would bring Mum home around four, by which time Peter was home. As long as I didn't go too far afield, I had time to walk, and get back to make tea. Mum often had a long nap on her return from her busy day so wasn't really aware that I had been away from home. My planned Lancashire walks were unearthed and I took off; walking over the wonderful red rose county of my birth. I walked over paths which criss-crossed various trails; The Pendle Witch Trail and the

Bronte Way being two notable ones. The trail markers of witches on their broomsticks made me smile as did the interesting rock formations and wide-reaching views on what was, new walking territory for me.

I was missing The Lakes but was still, slowly but surely increasing my hill count on go4awalk, where I carefully registered each summit that I reached. Boulsworth Hill, White Hill, Crutchenber Fell, Catlow Fell, (Raven's Castle), were all new names for me and the heathery terrain gave me more practise in navigation. These fells were quiet and gave me the head space I needed.

It was probably on one of these walks that I made the decision to retire at the end of the school year. Peter and I worked out that we would manage financially, with the carer's allowance and my teacher's pension coming in each month.

I was juggling work with my caring roles and although I was still enjoying my supply teaching and the intellectual challenges that it gave me, I was being pulled in too many directions. Leaving Mum in a morning was hard and her pleas for me not to go, would echo in my mind through the day, even though I knew that she would be fine as soon as I had gone. It pulled on my heartstrings, as leaving my children at Nursery had done over thirty years before.

I finished work at the end of term just after my fifty-ninth birthday.

As a supply teacher, I didn't expect anyone to mark my retirement in anyway and thought that I would just leave the school that I was working in that day and sign off with the agency. However, I did choose one of my favourite schools to work in for my last few days' teaching as a treat to myself. I was surprised and delighted when, on my last day, my dinner hour was interrupted, not my phone calls from Mum, but by members of the wonderful agency that I had worked for over thirteen years who came into the staffroom bearing flowers and some lovely gifts. I was very touched and it felt that I had been given a proper send-off, rather than just dropping off the radar after thirty- seven years in education.

By this time Mum was going to Memory Lane for two days a week and life became more balanced and I felt that I had time to breathe.

Mind you, Mum never did get used to the fact that I didn't need to get up at six o'clock in the morning once I was retired and would shout up the stairs at seven if I wasn't downstairs by then. Still, an early start did mean that I could the most of each day and give mum lots of attention. I would take her out somewhere special at least one day every week in an effort to keep her stimulated and keep the worst effects of her dementia at bay. Initially, she enjoyed choosing the destination. I would ask her where she fancied going and try to accommodate her wishes. A trip to the seaside at Filey and one to The Yorkshire Wildlife Park were two of her choices. The Filey outing was a trip down memory lane for her as she had been there as a child with her mum and sister to meet her dad when he was stationed at Catterick Garrison. It was lovely to see the joy on her face as she walked along the beach remembering happy childhood days out.

In August, I even managed to take her on coach trip to see my sister on The Isle of Wight for a few days. This wasn't the easiest of trips but it was lovely for her to be with her Isle of Wight family and spend some time with them.

Chapter 45.
Another GPS disaster and a close shave

Many walkers told me what a difference carrying a GPS (Global Positioning System) had made to their confidence on the hills. I couldn't get to grips with using one at all. Trying to follow a line on a screen didn't appeal. Often, when I had followed my compass on my chosen route, I would glance at my GPS and it would show that I was, supposedly, a distance off the path. Maybe, I should have bought a more expensive model or taken one of the many courses that were available in using one on the mountains but I really didn't feel that the benefits would add anything to my usual map and compass routine, used alongside the uncomplicated directions given on my go4awalk downloads.

I did give in to the pressure to replace my lost gadget, as it would allow me to give my exact position if I ever needed to call Mountain Rescue. I couldn't see me using it for anything else though. I didn't even buy a screen protector for my new GPS but, as I hadn't intending using it, I wasn't worried.

I had always believed that the wonderful Pendle Hill was the highest peak in Lancashire but I wanted to make sure that I had climbed to the highest point in the county of my birth so I logged into my computer to check. I was surprised to find that there were conflicting claims for this title. At one time, apparently, the highest was Coniston Old Man but then when boundaries were moved, the title was given to another mountain that I had climbed a few years previously, Gragareth. This and Green Hill, (lower by one foot), are inside the Lancashire boundary by only about two hundred metres.

I should have remembered that I had seen a Lancashire Boundary stone on that walk but because the walk, that I had downloaded, was in the Yorkshire Dales section of the Nuttalls, I hadn't realised that these fells were actually in Lancashire. Being reassured that I had climbed to the top of Lancashire, I looked for the next fell, height-wise, that had so far remained unclimbed. Ward's Stone or its alternative prettier name of Mallowdale Fell, was the next in height after Green Hill and the next in prominence after Pendle Hill so this seemed a good target for my next walk.

The weather wasn't brilliant, but as days for walking were few, I went anyway. I was warm and the paths were clear at the start of the walk but the cloud was quite low. I followed the track and then a fence to reach my first summit, the interestingly named Wolfhole Crag.

Wikipedia's entry for this fell doesn't make it sound the most attractive: -

Wolfhole Crag is a lonely and seldom-visited hill in the Forest of Bowland in Lancashire, England. Its seclusion is due in part to its low profile and long approach walks. A long path approaches from Ward's Stone in the west which is fraught with bogs.

Another comment I have found while researching the fell for this book found was more positive

Wolfhole Crag is one of the remotest and rockiest summits in the Forest of Bowland and is also quite possibly the best.

Even in this post though, there were these words which weren't exactly encouraging.

There are no clear paths to the summit and whichever

approach one takes, it is likely to be rough underfoot. This is particularly the case of the route from the eastern side of Ward's Stone. In places it is very peaty and while I was lucky enough to go this way following an extended dry spell, the remains of a recently deceased sheep stuck in a bog was a reminder that care still needed to be taken.

With these intriguing descriptions, I set off into the Lancashire hills. The weather soon deteriorated and when I had to stop to pull my rain-cover over my pack, I retrieved my Garmin from the depths of my rucksack. People had assured me that it would help me keep on track through bad weather and peat bogs. I turned it on and called up the route that I had put in the night before. Thankfully, I could see the little arrow, which showed my position, was on the line of the route I had planned.

I was walking after a period of dry weather so the peat wasn't too claggy but some of the drops into the groughs were quite deep. I wasn't particularly enjoying this walk but was determined to reach Ward's Stone. I was singing to myself to lift my spirits when I came across a particularly deep drop. I spotted a large stone sticking out of the peat, about halfway down the hag. I felt very lucky to have this natural step and thought that it would save me from jarring my knees as I jumped down.

I stepped onto the stone and the next thing I knew; I saw a large rock coming towards me as I dropped uncomfortably to my knees. Instinctively, I reached up to keep the rock from hitting my face. The rock knocked my glasses off as it glanced off the side of my cheek bone just below my eye. I was in a painful heap, in a peaty hole, scrambling around for my glasses making sure that I hadn't done much damage to myself. I had twisted my knee as I fell and I stretched it out tentatively in front of me and it didn't complain too much.

I found my glasses, which were also thankfully undamaged, and put them on, trying to avoid the bruising that I could already feel coming up on my cheek. I stood up and climbed out of the other side of the hole, looking back at the 'step', which I had been so thankful for minutes before, lying in its new home.

At least nobody else would be led into a false sense of security. I guessed that the recent dry spell had shrunk the peat around the stone and caused it to come loose as soon as I put my weight onto it. I hobbled on to Ward's Stone and ate my lunch, in the pouring rain, feeling very sorry for myself. I decided to look at my GPS for my onward route and saw that like me, it had been bruised and battered by my fall. 'Oh well!', I thought to myself,' I am obviously not meant to use one of these things on the fells.'

It was still working but was rather scratched. I did buy a protector for my GPS before my next walk but most of the time, it has remained out of sight in the emergency pocket of my rucksack along with my head-torch and jelly babies.

I took a look at my map and deciding that I had had enough for the day, I made my way down to the road instead of going on to bag Clougha Pike. I drove home feeling thankful to have dodged another disaster, rather than exhilarated by a walk in the glorious Lancashire Hills.

Chapter 46.
Another challenge or just a good ending?

In spite of the occasional hair-raising moment, I was enjoying my occasional outing to explore new territory but was missing having something to aim for. I had no desire to complete all the Dewey's, and I certainly didn't want to get to the point where we were planning holidays around them. I would finish those in The Lake District and if I could bag some close to home then so be it.

I had reached a total of five hundred different fells while I was climbing the Nuttalls in 2017, when I had trudged over peat hags to reach a fallen and damaged Trig point on the summit of Meldon Hill in the North Pennines. There was no champagne or friends to share the moment but I had been pleased to think back on my adventures that day, as I descended over High Cup Nick.

I realised that it was less than a year to my sixtieth birthday and that I would have to accept that my walking days would be few as Mum and Peter were needing me at home more and more.

Since Meldon Hill, I had climbed well over sixty fells, so I suddenly had a light bulb moment. Being a lover of neat numbers, I wondered whether I would be able to reach a total of six hundred different summits before I was sixty. I had another peak bagging challenge that could be done on any hills that I could reach and climb while Peter was at work and mum being cared for. There was no list to follow. This challenge was purely personal. It would also be a nice tidy number to finish on if my caring role or my arthritis prevented serious walking in the future. I was bagging peaks with a purpose once again.

Peter and I did have a week's holiday in the North Lakes in September, in an accessible apartment, while my sister cared for Mum. Peter even joined me on the summit of a fell; Binsey. An amazing company called Freedom Wizard advertised, on Facebook, that they had all terrain mobility vehicles which could access a few of the lower Wainwright Fells. I contacted them and arranged for a voucher to be sent to Peter for his birthday which would entitle him to an outing in one of their 'Bomber' vehicles. This was planned for the Tuesday of our holiday. The day had started off damp but the rain stopped and the sun shone as we reached the foot of Binsey and Peter was helped into his transport by the three people who were going to join us on our ascent. There had been a problem charging the vehicle and there was some apprehension about whether it would reach the top but we set off in good faith. Our progress was slow, but it gave us time to enjoy the views expanding below us.

Although the bomber couldn't make it over the last few rocky yards to the trig point, with four of us to help and encourage him, Peter made his way determinedly to the top using his sticks. The joy on our faces, as I joined him for a photograph is evident. I had tears in my eyes as we stood together looking at the hills of Scotland in the distance and Lakeland Fells and Derwentwater below us. This was one walk that I wouldn't have to share with Peter only through pictures on my computer. It did make us wish that we could have more days like that but it was one we wouldn't ever forget.

I climbed a few new Dewey's that week but Peter and I also enjoyed other sights in the Northern Lakes and relaxed for the first time in ages. It was particularly fun for me to know that the week we had chosen for our

Peter and Me Together on Binsey Summit
September 2018

holiday was the first week of term and that for the first time in thirty-seven years, it didn't matter.

We returned home refreshed and I was able to spend quality time with Mum during the day without worrying about school.

The following month, I was going to be taking up another caring role; one which would be a sheer joy. My daughter, Rebecca and her husband Tom, had for several months been trying to sell their house in Berkhamsted, with the intention of moving closer to both sets of grandparents. They had a problem with their buyer and ended up having to reach an agreement with their mortgage provider that they would rent out their lovely home for two years. As Tom had secured a job in Leeds, they had to vacate their house and move North without anywhere to live. Luckily, there was room for them in Tom's parent's home. Rebecca was then able to find work as an accountant at Asda House in Leeds for when she finished her maternity leave.

In October, when Rebecca started her new job, we established a new routine. Rebecca would put Bertie into a nursery near work on Wednesday and then would drive to our house with him after work and I would prepare a meal for us all. Rebecca would then go off to work on Thursday leaving me to look after my gorgeous grandson. Having a baby around was also good for Mum. It was amazing to see them together and over the months that he was coming to us, they became as thick as thieves. Rebecca's routine gave Tom's mum a bit of a break as she was doing the bulk of looking after the little family.

Again, my days were becoming busy but I wouldn't have changed the special family times I was having even though it wasn't easy.

My Wolfhole Crag adventure hadn't put me off the

Lancashire Fells and I was happy to climb more. I found several walks to wonderfully named fells like Paddy's Pole, Parlick and Bull Hill. I also came across pretty Lancashire villages; Chipping was a particular favourite. I climbed to the summits of Paddy's Pole and Parlick from this lovely sleepy village in December of 2018. I walked in a chilly breeze but the winter sun was bright and lit up the distant views and even the muddy puddles shone, reflecting the cornflower blue sky which was striped with wispy white clouds. The walk was short and I moved quickly to keep warm so had plenty of time to wander round the cobbled streets on my return to Chipping a village which time seems to have forgotten. I was captured by its charm and wandered for a while reading the various plaques and admiring the beautiful church and ancient waterwheel before driving home and back to the present day.

One area that I had avoided walking was Saddleworth Moor between The Peak District and the West Pennine Moors. As a child growing up in the 1960s, Saddleworth Moor always seemed bleak and carried a sense of foreboding. This was the result of the horrendous child murders carried out by Myra Hindley and Ian Brady between 1963 and 1965.

We had driven over the M62, looking at these unwelcoming hills, numerous times, on visits to the cottage from Leeds and I had never once looked at them with the desire that I felt when viewing other fells from the confines of the car. However, having climbed several Lancashire Fells, I widened my search to include Greater Manchester. I looked at the map and realised that many of the walks for that area would taking me onto the moors that I had previously had no desire to set foot on.

I drove over the M62 turning off at the exit for

Saddleworth Moor, not sure what to expect. I had a day of contrasts but a day that finally rid me of the feeling of gloom on seeing that sign. The walk caused me no problems but it is not often that you climb to a summit and find that it is topped with a small wind-farm as Rough Hill in the South Pennines is. The next summit, Freeholds Top had a small but pretty pool decorating the area near the trig point. However, it was I approached the final summit of the day, Brown Wardle Hill that I realised that this area didn't need to be defined by the evil of the past. I walked towards the hill and as I did, I was aware that this was a busy ridge. I was the only hiker for miles around but I was surrounded by beautiful fell ponies, swishing their thick manes over their dense coats which would protect them from the worst of the winter winds. Most of the ponies were completely black and there was one white pony and a young black and white foal but the animal that drew my eye was a rich copper with a contrasting black mane. He obligingly turned towards me and posed for a photograph. As I took that picture, that wonderful animal was unaware that seeing him had allowed me to lay a lot of ghosts to rest and now, when I drive over the cross Pennine motorway, I remember that wild, innocent creature that made my spirits soar.

The Peak District also knew the tread of my boots over first six months of 2019. I loved discovering the interesting rock formations and ticking off a few more Dewey's in that area to get my total fell count nearer to six hundred. I even managed to bag a fell that had caused problems for the great walker, Alfred Wainwright,

The author Alfred Wainwright described Black Hill as 'a brute in any weather' and advised walkers to be prepared for a tough and gruelling trek.

'Nothing can grow in this acid waste,' he wrote. 'There is no root-hold in this sea of ooze. In the flutings and ripplings of the surface of the dunes caused by the action of rain and wind, a certain strange beauty, a patterned sculpturing beyond the skill of man, must, however, be conceded. But it is a frightening place in bad weather, a dangerous place after heavy rain. It is not a place to visit unaccompanied.'

In fact, he had to be rescued from some deep boot sucking peat on that very fell, being pulled bodily from the quagmire by his walking friend. In his Pennine Way Companion, Wainwright gives this warning.

'Before resuming the journey, (from Black Hill), look around to make sure there is nobody sinking out of sight and in need of help.'

I was lucky when I went in January 2019 as there has been a lot of peat conservation work in that area and there are helpful flagstones to the summit so my feet stayed dry. I was able to walk easily to the summit from Wessenden Head on the Kirklees Way and back on the Pennine Way via Black Moss and Wessenden reservoirs. It was a bitterly cold day but even on this winter's day the hill could happily now be called Green Hill, its black peat now covered with healthy foliage. Congratulations to all who are working to conserve these wonderful peat moorlands.

I found rocks and summits with wonderful names in The Peak District; Black Chew Head, Featherbed Moss, Cat's Tor, Mount Famine to name but a few and visited some places that I had heard of but never seen, Stanage Edge being one of them.

The only problem was that no matter how many wonderful views I saw and walks I enjoyed, my route

Wild ponies on the fells above the M62 April 2019

back home from these fells was on the M1 or the M62. I didn't feel as rested or energised as with my Lake District Walks from which I pootled home along the very pretty A65 which always seemed shorter because it was so familiar.

I had to accept it; I was hefted to Lakeland.

Wainwright's words rung very true to me: -

'*Surely there is no other place in this whole wonderful world quite like Lakeland... no other so exquisitely lovely, no other so charming, no other that calls so insistently across a gulf of distance. All who truly love Lakeland are exiles when away from it.*'

Still, my six hundredth fell was getting closer and I was still getting out on hills occasionally, so I couldn't complain.

Chapter 47.
Answers for Peter at last

Twenty years after Peter had started having mobility issues, he was finally able to have a genetic test that would give him the answers he wanted. The test proved that he had Hereditary Spastic Paraplegia.

The family history of mobility problems had been unclear and indecisive; certainly nobody, as far as the family knew, had symptoms as severe as Peter. It was of course good to have a definite diagnosis at last but of course, this raised questions for our daughters.

They then had to have genetic testing themselves and of course, Rebecca and Tom were worried about Bertie and by the time she was being tested, Rebecca was pregnant with our granddaughter. Both girls had an anxious wait, especially Rebecca as the lab lost her bloods and she had to have the test done again. Thankfully, both girls tested negative and Rebecca could enjoy her pregnancy and she and Tom could watch Bertie, learning to run and climb, without watching for stumbling steps that might point to him having HSP too. They also knew that there was no danger of their children passing it on to future generations.

About the time of Peter's diagnosis, I noticed a wonderful charity in the Lakes raising money for Multiple Sclerosis. The 10 in 10 Challenge, urges people to raise sponsorship by climbing ten mountains in ten hours. I contacted the charity and asked if I could also use the challenge to raise money for the HSP support group, as well as the required amount for Multiple Sclerosis, which would use money to look deeper into this horrible condition. They readily agreed as both HSP and MS are neurological conditions and any research in this area could potentially help both.

I was also given six weeks respite for Mum, which I could use between April 2019 and April 2020. Apparently, I had been entitled to the same the previous year but no one had told me! I found a lovely care home that agreed to take her for three weeks. It seemed a long time for her but they assured me that three weeks was less unsettling than a short stay. Carers Leeds also offer carers an occasional sum of two hundred and fifty pounds. I decided to use the money to book myself into a lovely bed and breakfast in Littletown near the start of the walk and booked Mum in for her first spell of respite.

I was going back to my beloved Lakes and would have three days walking including, possibly, one of the hardest day's walking I had ever done.

I had two Dewey's left to do in The Lake District and I could do these on short walks to warm up my legs for the big challenge on the 22nd of June. This would leave me only two fells to do to reach a total of six hundred different fells before my sixtieth birthday less than a month after the challenge.

On the seventeenth of June, a Monday, I took time to settle Mum into the care home. The staff were lovely and Mum seemed to understand that she was just staying for a short time to give me a break. Unfortunately, she obviously hadn't understood as much as I thought and kept packing her case ready to come home. Still after a couple of days, she had got used to the routine and I felt that she was calm enough for me to head to The Lakes on the Thursday.

I managed to climb to the summit of Black Crags, Langdale, revelling in the wonderful views down Mickleden, before heading for Littletown. It was a good leg stretch but I didn't feel that I had over done it. The next day I had an even smaller fell in mind and drove to Whinlatter Forest to have a steady walk to Ullister Hill. I felt I was ready for my Ten in Ten Challenge.

You may be wondering about my arthritis at this point. I was still in pain, even though the treatment I was having had made a big difference. However, it was what my lovely rheumatologist said, as much as the treatment that I was on, that kept me walking. She said, 'What you have to remember with arthritis, is that pain doesn't equate to damage.'

Usually, pain tells our bodies to take action to avoid it; think about how quickly you move your hand from a hot surface or jump away if you stand on something sharp. With arthritis, you are in pain but if you can get that under control then exercise is the best thing you can do, as strengthening the muscles around the damaged joints will support them.

A physiotherapist had also explained why I felt less pain when walking alone than being led in a group. She said that our bodies are wonderfully made and that if we need to concentrate on our survival, then pain signals can be muted. This helped me to understand why, at the end of a walk when I was on a clear path back to the car, the last mile or so always seemed so painful.

Knowing these things helped me to push myself though pain to enjoy my walking, sometimes helped by paracetamol and anti-inflammatory gels.

Chapter 48.
The 10 in 10 Challenge

I was nervous as I chatted to other guests in the B&B who were also taking part in the challenge. One chap that I spoke to, was one of the organisers and, offered to take me to the start in his car which would save me adding miles to the sixteen or so I would be walking. (I didn't worry at this point about how I would get back at the end of the day.) I asked the proprietors if I could make some porridge the next morning; always my breakfast of choice, as we would be gone before the official breakfast time. I didn't get a lot of sleep but woke up on the day of the walk feeling ready to go but also wondering if I was capable of this challenge. I had managed to raise a lot of sponsorship and didn't want to let people down.

We left the B&B before five but the time soon passed until we were off, an hour and a half later. I was glad that we were starting so early as it was forecast to be a very hot day so I was glad to do the first big climb in the cooler morning air. The first ascent was a steep one and took a lot longer than I was anticipating. Initially, I was a bit worried about timing but then I realised that the next four fells wouldn't have such long ascents. I had done the bulk of the climbing for the first half of the walk. I was also encouraged by those around me; in particular two seventeen-year-old girls who had offered to carry my poles while I scrambled to the summit of Rowling End just before reaching the short ridge to Causey Pike. It was lovely to keep catching sight of them and realising that if I was keeping up with them, then I wasn't doing too badly.

The marshals on top of each summit checked us in and replenished our energy with a ready supply of flapjack and jelly babies. I wasn't walking as a team or with friends, as many were, but I felt well supported as I walked from summit to summit. It didn't seem too long before I was making the steep descent into Buttermere. This wasn't my favourite part of the day as the path seemed endless and knowing that we would have to climb again, as soon as we got down, didn't help. I watched the fell runners who were taking part bouncing past me down the hill. I decided that I would take a leaf out of their book and began jogging a little when I got to a grassy part of the descent. It did help and at least I covered the ground more quickly than I had been doing. It was lovely to reach Buttermere where we could visit the loo and refuel at the station set up for this purpose. There were lots of cakes and pieces of fruit as well as drinks.

I had learnt from previous long walks not to stop too long though or I knew that I would struggle to get going again so after a few minutes I was climbing again. The climb up to the summit of Robinson via High Snockrigg is long and relentless but I took it steadily and was even able to encourage another walker who was struggling on this section. By the time I reached Robinson summit, I had seven out of ten mountains under my belt. The next fell was one I was familiar with as I had done it several times; Dale Head. What I hadn't remembered were how many false the summits there were before I reached the true top. There was then another steep descent; this time, I didn't even bother making the effort to jog or walk down. I decided that my legs needed a rest and I went down the majority of the slope on my bottom. There were people looking at me strangely but I didn't care. I got down by shuffling, walking only when this wasn't possible. When I finally stood up again my legs were ready to go knowing that there were only two fells left.

For a brief moment, as I walked towards High Spy from Dale Head Tarn I was on my own. It was a special moment as being alone on the fells is always magical for me but not something that I expected in such a busy event. Mind you, I was relieved when I did spot someone ahead to assure me that I wasn't on my own because I had taken the wrong path.

Before long I had reached the final summit of the day, Maiden Moor. This was a peak that I had climbed with Rebecca as a warm up for the following day when I took her up Scafell Pike. I also have a picture of myself on Maiden Moor from that wonderful holiday in 1972 when I fell in love with The Lake District. Who knew then that I would be there again nearly forty-eight years later.

What I hadn't appreciated was just how far I would have to walk from that last summit back to The Swinside Inn where we would register our time and get our certificate. Once again, I had to find reserves from somewhere. I was on my own for much of the road walking and I could happily have sat down by the side of the road and thumbed a lift. I kept plodding as the white building grew closer. As I came within sight of people waiting at the entrance gate of the pub, they started whistling and ringing cow bells. It was just the support I needed and I sped up for the last hundred yards or so. After checking in and being given a time of just over nine hours with which I was delighted I called Peter. I simply said, 'I'm at The Swinside Inn.' His reply brought tears to my eyes, 'So am I!'

I couldn't believe it. Peter had driven up from Leeds. He was hoping to be there to cheer me in but that had proved difficult as he had had to park in Keswick and get a taxi to the inn. It was wonderful to see him. There was an evening of music and a barbecue for participants at The Swinside but to be honest, the thought of a bath, a change of clothes and quiet meal with Peter was far more appealing. I was too tired to socialise. So, we got a taxi back to Keswick for Peter's car and he took me back to Littletown so I could get cleaned up, he had even brought me some special bubble bath. We then drove down to The Fish in Buttermere for a lovely relaxed dinner. I didn't really want to say goodbye to him when he took me back to Littletown but I would be driving straight home, after a good night's sleep, to see him again the following day.

Five days after the 10 in10, while Mum was still in respite, Peter drove me up the M6 to climb a fell that I had spotted at the side of the motorway on my many drives up to the Lakes; Grayrigg Forest. It took us a while to find the lay-by from which I could start walking but it didn't take me long to climb to the summit of my five hundred and ninety-ninth fell.

Chapter 49.
Six hundred fells at sixty

Mum was due home from respite on the eighth of July so we organised a trip to the summit of Beacon Fell for the day before. I was delighted that my lovely family and my childhood friend, Helen, and her husband were going to join me along with Peter in a Tramper which we had booked from the visitors' centre.

Beacon Fell was a gentle walk for me but, for my six-hundredth fell celebration, it was perfect. Tom and Rebecca were able to bring Bertie, confident that, with a bit of help and encouragement, he could walk up the good track by himself, especially with the distraction of carved snakes and owls on the way for him to look at. Poor Hannah had been diagnosed with the painful condition, fibromyalgia, so this walk was probably at the limits of what she could manage at the time but with the help of her lovely partner Matt, she made it. Helen and Alan weren't mountain walkers but enjoyed this type of walking so steadily, we all made our way to the top. Peter had brought the obligatory champagne in the tramper and I was able to celebrate my achievement with the people who had made it possible. Without their support, I would never have started peak bagging and certainly wouldn't have had so many adventures. I love every one of them dearly and having them to come home to was very special.

I had made it with two weeks to spare! Since my decision to climb the highest fifty Wanwright's, fourteen years earlier, I had: -

Climbed over eight hundred fells (several of which included repeats of favourite rounds);

Walked over three thousand hill miles;

Climbed over four hundred and sixty thousand feet;

Worn out three pairs of hiking boots and two pairs of walking poles.

Although I had walked and climbed with some lovely people, over 750 fells had been climbed solo.

None of this would have been possible without support from family who had allowed me to pursue my crazy peak bagging hobby.

I celebrated my sixtieth birthday a fortnight later. The design of the cake, made by a friend of mine, was no surprise but wonderful all the same. It was topped with sugar paste models of a cairn, walking boots, a map, walking poles and a signpost.

I didn't have a big party but the people who helped me to celebrate were friends and family who meant so much to me, including my lovely mum who enjoyed meeting people and certainly had more than her allotted share of macarons, as did Bertie. I think they conspired to finish them off between them.

I knew that after all the celebrations, most of my time would be spent caring for Mum, Peter and Bertie. I also wanted to support Hannah, as she struggled to balance exercise and rest to manage the pain of her fibromyalgia, while studying for a degree. Matt was brilliant but he worked away two days a week.

Rebecca had announced that her and Tom were expecting a daughter in March of 2020, so the knitting needles would be out again.

There was also going to be another exciting event at the end of 2019. Hannah and Matt were going to celebrate their relationship in a quiet civil ceremony on the first day that mixed sexed Civil Partnerships became legal. I would be making a cake for the celebration with friends and family on the day after the ceremony. With all these ways to fill my days, I didn't need to find anything else.

I did manage one or two walks before the end of the year but these were few and far between. I didn't feel restless; I had completed all the challenges I had set myself and was more than happy to dedicate my time to helping those I love and who had done so much to support me. They would always come first.

However, on one of these walks, from Haweswater, with my friend Jenny, she took a snap of me as we climbed the steep ridge of The Rigg to High Street. When the picture was uploaded onto Facebook, Peter captioned it with the words, 'Truly at home'. He knew that part of my heart would always be on the mountains in The Lake District.

Chapter 50.
Walking in the dark

On the last of my 2019 walks, I had to face a problem that I had avoided until then; walking in the dark. I was tempted as usual by a wonderful forecast. It was the last day of November, so I knew I wouldn't have a lot of light but I set off for Honister Slate Mine, to climb Great Gable (thinking that there may be plenty of people about), very early in the morning. The sun was rising above Derwentwater as I drove into the Borrowdale Valley. I parked up at Honister and took photographs of some amazing views looking glorious in the pink of the dawn.

I climbed Grey Knotts and Brandreth keeping a good pace on the steep ascent to fend off the cold. The winter sun reflecting off icy pools and snow-covered peaks made me so glad that I had made the effort to be there. As I walked towards Green Gable, I looked across to Base Brown. It looked magnificent and drew me towards it. I walked to its summit and took an unusual picture of the fell lit up by the sun under a curtain of the dark cloud of twilight which was just starting to descend. The colours were incredible.

I turned and started up the paths to Green Gable and Great Gable. As I expected, there were at least half a dozen other walkers on the summit. The top was bleaker than the rest of the walk had been. It was bitterly cold with a thick frost. I didn't hang around as I was eager to get down to the path back to Honister in good light. I should have headed back down to Windy Gap but had made the decision to get down to Moses Tod straight from the top of Great Gable as I was following a small group but they were soon racing ahead as they were hoping to bag Kirk Fell, before they turned back. I started the descent and suddenly had the most horrendous cramp. I couldn't put any weight on my right leg at all.

As the group disappeared from sight, I had to sit and shuffle down the scree slope. Even this was painful, so my progress was very slow. I did try to stand from time to time but the steepness of the path set the cramp off again. Finally, I was on the route to the Coast-to-Coast path, Moses Trod, back to the slate mine. Standing up on level ground gave my leg the stretch it needed and the cramp faded. Unfortunately, so did the light. I had a quick packet of crisps and donned my extra clothes and head-torch, hoping I could make good progress before darkness.

I only had minutes though, before I realised that darkness was closing in on me. Even though I was on a good path, the ground was icy and I was worried that if I fell, I would risk becoming hypothermic very quickly. I had two and a half miles to walk and there was not a soul to be seen. I was scared but I knew that I had to keep moving.

After a while, following my torch beam and my compass, celebrating the sight of every cairn showing I was on the path, I decided that I would phone Mountain Rescue. I didn't want them to come out but I thought that I would be able to give them my location and explain what I was doing. I did hope that someone could perhaps check in with me every quarter of an hour or so to check out that I was okay. I tried! My phone hadn't even got a signal for emergency numbers. I tried my whistle, in the hope that someone might answer. My whistle sounded out, loud and clear in the night air but there was no whistle in reply. Oh well! There was nothing for it but to keep going.

I was so happy when I reached the Drum House, part of the dismantled railway track from the mine on Fleetwith Pike. It confirmed that I was on the correct route and that I was nearly back at the car park. As I reached the steep steps down to the buildings of the slate mine, now in darkness, I could see a security light glowing eerily on the youth hostel next door. The steps were, by this time, covered in ice so I held on tightly to the rusty wire fence and intermittent wooden posts as I made my descent. I had a brief rest from the effort and located my car key. I hopefully pressed the button and grinned from ear to ear as, below me, my car lit up, looking no less impressive than Blackpool Illuminations.

I had got myself out of trouble once again! If I was a cat, I think I would have used all of my nine lives.

Why couldn't I just be satisfied with a gentle stroll round the park?

As Christmas approached, I thought that my caring role was taking its toll, I felt very tired. I then went down with a terrible cold and cough. I took myself to the GP and was given antibiotics for a chest infection. By the middle of the week after Christmas, I still felt so poorly that I rang the care home to see if they could take Mum. I didn't want her catching anything but neither did I have the energy to care for her. They told me to bring her straight down as they could hear how ill I sounded.

After a couple of days treatment and a good rest, I felt more like myself and was able to enjoy Hannah and Matt's special day which went exactly as they wanted it. The ceremony was attended only by Rebecca and a close mutual friend as witnesses. I then took them for a celebratory lunch and Peter and I joined them with others on the following day for an informal party with their friends and Matt's family.

By the first weekend in January, I was recovering from my chest infection and Peter had gone back to work. I had been following some walking groups on Facebook but had never joined any of their walks. However, one group evented a gentle walk which said that it was suitable for children. I decided that I would join them while trying to regain my fitness.

I met some lovely people and indeed many people from this group; Head4theHills, have since become friends.

It was on this walk, up Troutbeck Tongue, that John, one of the leaders and administrators of the group, was chatting to me and asked me how many Wainwright's I had done more than once. I said I had no idea but that I would have a look.

As we walked up the valley towards the small fell, a rainbow appeared; its intense colours painting the slopes of Wansfell, before it faded into the landscape. I was enraptured by the view. The feelings that I had for the Lake District that day were as strong that day as on my early visits over fifty years before.

When I got home, I started to tot up my Wainwright count; I had done over eighty fells twice and some more than that.

The following week there was another walk in the same area, climbing the three other Troutbeck Fells, Sour Howes, Sallows and Baystones', (the Wainwright summit of Wansfell). I got chatting to John again and he asked if I had thought about completing a second round. I had to admit I was tempted. However, this was January 2020 and we were all unaware of how much our lives were to change in just two short months as the pandemic took hold.

Did I give in to temptation when we were released from Lockdown?

Well, that's another story.

Thanks and Acknowledgements

My first thanks must be to my wonderful family: -

To Peter for encouraging my solo exploits and always being there to come home to.

To Hannah and Rebecca for being the best daughters any mum could have and for the joy they bring me every day.

To my late mum and dad for instilling in me a love of the outdoors and for trusting me on those early hostelling holidays.

I would also like to thank the people who have played a part in helping me to find my way over the many mountains, fells and hills that I have climbed: -

The leaders of the CHA, especially George, who taught me to love and respect the fells.

Wainwright for his wonderful Pictorial Guides and inspirational words that made me want to follow in his footsteps.

The creators of the website go4walk.com, without whose help I would never have undertaken so many challenges. Their directions have helped to keep me safe in the hills.

Alan Pearson for helping me to climb Pillar Rock and to Mike Dawson who joined me and encouraged me to complete this challenge.

John and Anne Nuttall for their book which encouraged me into new mountainous areas of England, and onto fells that I had never even heard of.

The many volunteers who keep the fell paths in good condition and the farmers who tolerate my presence on their land.

The Mountain Rescue teams who give up their time so selflessly to support those who walk the fells.

The Rheumatology Team at Harrogate Hospital, especially Dr Helen MacIver and Sister Lynsey Hall for their advice, sympathy and determination to keep me walking.

Finally, I would like to thank all those friends who have patiently listened to my many tales of walking and climbing and who told me that I should write a book. Well, here it is; I hope you enjoy it.

About the Author

Christine Shepherd was born in Bolton, Lancashire. She now lives in Yorkshire with her husband, Peter. She has two daughters, Hannah and Rebecca, and is granny to two wonderful grandchildren. She is a retired teacher who has a passion for reading as well as walking the fells. This is her first book and is the result of many requests to write down the exciting memories that she has shared with friends.